THE **DEAD** PROPHETS SOCIETY

MARK CHIRONNA

The Dead Prophets Society

by Mark Chironna
copyright ©2018

Trade paperback ISBN: 978-1-943294-76-3
Cover design by Mario Hood

CONTENTS

FOREWORD

JOHN RECORDS JESUS' FAREWELL DISCOURSE in John 14–16. The Farewell Discourse is a series of teachings Jesus gives to his disciples in preparing them for his future ascension. When Jesus was preparing his disciples for his upcoming death, resurrection, and then departure back to the Father, he made some startling comments and then offered an assuring promise. Jesus said it was better for them if he would leave because the Father would send another, the Holy Spirit, to remind them of his teachings and to guide them into all truth.

One thing for sure, Jesus did not promise his disciples a book; that is, he did not say, "Do not worry about the future for I will make sure you have a book that will tell you everything you need to know and do." What he did say was, "The Counselor, the Holy Spirit, whom the Father will send in my name, will teach you all things and will remind you of everything I have said to you" (John 14:26 NIV). Furthermore, Jesus said that the Holy Spirit would guide them. The Holy Spirit, of course, is the Spirit of Christ and enables every believer to become part of a priestly and prophetic community in service to the mission of Christ.

We all appreciate that we have an inspired book, the Holy Bible! We understand that it is the penultimate authority in our community; however, the Bible alone will not suffice. Jesus said it is better for us to have the Holy Spirit, who illuminates Scripture and creates a charismatic-pentecostal community—a prophethood of believers. Jesus' Church, however, is in need of renewal and restoration. The Church is in need of Spirit-filled prophets and prophetesses. More than buildings filled with people listening to the reading of Scripture, God is looking for people filled with the Spirit—people with a prophetic perception charting a course of action in these last days. God is longing for prophetic communities who understand the Scriptures and discern the times in which we are living so that they might participate in creating the best possible future for creation.

Bishop Dr. Mark J. Chironna's monograph is borne out of prophetic prayer for the restoration of the Church through the formation of a prophetic people. In this work, Dr. Chironna lays out a manifesto for how this restoration can take place. The heart of it is that the people of God would truly embrace their divine calling to be the priests and prophets who understand the times in which they live, so that they would engage in the divine mission with God in shaping the future in decisive ways. In doing so they become true daughters and sons of Issachar, a prophetic-charismatic tribe that perceives the hand of the Father working in these last days. Moved by discerning rightly, the prophetic community joins the sacred Trinity in restoring and rebuilding the sacred City—the Church of the Living God.

"God still saves, delivers, heals, sanctifies, speaks, and leads. He is not only the God of history," Chironna writes, "but the God of our times and our children's times." The good news is that God "cannot be restrained by evil or discouraged by sin. He is always powerful and always eager to work in and through a prophetic people who see and act in accordance with His will." Such a prophetic people must see the present opportunities for restoration and rebuilding. In order for the sons and daughters of Issachar to see possibility and alternative outcomes, they *must* pay close attention to how God worked in the past, be saturated in the sacred Scriptures, and be led by the Holy Spirit as they stay connected to and rooted in Christ.

Such a community of Christ's followers is empowered to discern the hand of the Triune God working and shaping the events of their times for God's glory and creation's redemption, especially humanity. The Church as God's prophetic vanguard company is to be dedicated to restoring others rather than protecting itself. The Church is to honor the Father by following the Spirit and living like the Jesus, instead of promoting themselves, following deceptive spirits (which always encourage destruction, wantonness, sin, and subjugation), and living like worldly entertainers.

It does not take a prophetic people to see what everyone else sees—upheaval, uncertainty, amorality—but the daughters and sons of Issachar interpret these signs differently. When others focus on lack and doom, becoming ever more selfish and stingy, the true authentic prophetic community is about their Father's business. They are selflessly restoring the city of God by creating an alternative community, a refuge for the broken and oppressed, a city of shalom, which is Christ's Church.

Becoming a prophetic Church requires a people with a prophetic imagination. This is not easy. This monograph will not offer a simple three-step formula for success. But what it does offer is a pathway to becoming a prophetic people. Bishop Chironna offers the reader an opportunity to develop a prophetic imagination so that she/he might begin to see what the Spirit is doing, and join in the restoration of the Church.

I encourage you to read this work and heed what the Spirit is saying to the churches in these last days and in doing so, you will embark upon a journey discerning the invisible hand of God working in shaping the events of our times. In the words of Bishop Dr. Chironna, "The past will not be changed. It *cannot* be changed. But when we understand the times that are past and accurately perceive the present time and the times in which we live, we will know how to seize the future for the sake of Jesus."

Kenneth J. Archer, PhD (University of St Andrews)
Professor of Theology and Pentecostal Studies
Southeastern University
Lakeland, Florida

PREFACE

ONE OF THE MOST POIGNANT roles played by the late actor Robin Williams is that of the fictional John Keating, an unorthodox English teacher in an elite all-boys school in Vermont. The movie is *Dead Poets Society,* and the story takes place at Welton Academy in 1959.

John Keating's intent is to inspire students as he teaches them poetry. So on the first day of classes he utters an eye-opening exhortation, "Make your lives extraordinary," and adds the Latin phrase carpe diem, from Roman poet, Horace. Taken literally, the expression means "pluck the day." Today, we would say, "Seize the day."

Among the poems Keating reads to his class is Walt Whitman's "O Captain! My Captain!" a metaphorical treatment of Abraham Lincoln's assassination. Keating explains that Whitman wrote the poem as a eulogy, knowing that the slain president would never see the impact of his life on history. Through the poem, Whitman gave the deceased president a voice. Through his teaching, Keating gave Whitman's voice to his students—and rallied them to make their lives extraordinary!

John Keating had himself been a Welton student and a member of the Dead Poets Society, an unsanctioned secret club. One of his students found out about the club and decided to restart it. Inspired by their engagement with now dead poets, the boys dared to "pluck the day," each in his own unique way. However, pressing the boundaries of man-made traditions also created unrest. Sadly, one of the boys took his own life, and John Keating lost his job.

The movie's life lessons are profound and make us aware that the impact of poets cannot be contained by the times in which they live. As generation after generation engages with the power of poetic speech, even long-dead poets' words ring true, unleashing potential and possibility in the hearts of those who truly hear what the poets said.

Poetry and prophecy were often inseparable in the ancient world. A glance through the multitudes of Scripture passages shows how profoundly poetic the ancient prophets' utterances were. Rich in metaphor, their words sank deep into the hearts of their hearers, shaping their perspectives and altering their understanding of reality in favor of a Yahweh-shaped worldview. In the words of nineteenth-century professor Dr. Edward Pollard, "The prophet, like the true poet, must have inspiration; and while not striving after form, yet, seeing clearly and feeling deeply, he must sing. When the truth is fired with feeling, poetry is inevitable."[1]

What occurs in the lives of the prophets includes speech-acts, dramatic presentations, and the like. On his deathbed, Jacob prophesied with the laying on of hands over all twelve of his sons. Consider for a moment his prophecy to his son Issachar:

Issachar is a strong donkey, lying down between the sheep-folds. When he saw that a resting place was good and that the land was pleasant, he bowed his shoulder to bear burdens, and became a slave at forced labor.[2]

This prophetic utterance by Jacob is a concealed Messianic prophecy. While the text contains poetic ambiguities, the unpacking of its metaphors offers clues to its actual meaning. Over the course of their history, the sons of Issachar would become known both for their prophetic perception in "reading"

---

1. Edward B. Pollard, PhD, "The Prophet as a Poet," in *The Biblical World,* ed. William R. Harper (Chicago: University of Chicago Press, 1898), 4:327.

2. Gen. 49:14–15.

the times and their awareness of what needed to be done as a result.[3] According to Jewish orthodoxy, they were Torah scholars,[4] and while they were not the only tribe from which prophets came, they pointed ultimately to Christ, about whom Moses prophesied.[5] He is the fulfillment of every metaphor of Israel's twelve tribes and the True Spirit-Inspired Son of Issachar, who understands the times and knows what to do.[6]

In the reign of kings from Saul onward, the prophet is cast as the king's right-hand advisor and closest confidant. During a period of decline when the testimony of Yahweh was in need of recovery, a man of priestly descent named Elijah was raised up to address Ahab and Jezebel, who were hostile to the prophet's voice. Elijah's battles with princes and powers were intense; immediately after his greatest victory, he experienced a deep, inner, personal defeat.[7]

Yahweh's prescription for healing his prophet was to give him a gift—an emerging prophetic voice from Abel-meholah, in Issachar territory. There a true son of Issachar diligently plowed the field so it could receive fresh seed. This was Elisha, the son of Shaphat, who became Elijah's heir apparent.

Much has been said about how Elisha had no one to whom he could pass his mantle. Speculation abounds when preachers claim that he failed to reproduce himself. These conjectures accomplish little in relation to understanding and "rightly dividing the word of truth."[8] Perhaps we need to realize that the Law, the Prophets, and the Wisdom literature *all* point to Jesus, and

---

3. 1 Chron. 12:32.

4. David S. Zinberg, "Re-imagining Issachar," *Ideals Institute for Jewish Ideas and Ideals,* accessed March 28, 2018, https://www.jewishideas.org/article/re-imagining-issachar.

5. Deut. 18:15; Acts 3:22.

6. Matt. 16:1–4.

7. 1 Kings 19.

8. 2 Tim. 2:15.

every type and shadow contained within them necessarily falls short of the glory of God, which is Christ Himself.

I contend that Elisha did not fail, but had a successor. Our inability to discern the real message of his death and his dead bones is at the core of what *Dead Prophets Society* is all about.

Robin Williams's John Keating character claimed that occupations are "noble pursuits and necessary to sustain life,"[9] but passion is the reason to live. Like his prophetic predecessor, Elisha passionately pursued the living God. In the end, he died not only of a sickness, but also of a broken heart when the king to whom he was assigned failed to respond in full obedience to his prophetic word. Because of his sinful self-interest, the king complied outwardly, with little or no passion. As a result, a few short-lived victories dissolved into ongoing enemy oppression.[10]

Elisha was buried with no fanfare, in a shared public grave which was more than likely a cave-tomb. His unlikely successor was destined to be a dead person, young and having died before his time, who never lived out his destiny and never made his life extraordinary. As far as the reader is concerned, this young man is unknown and unnamed, and is tossed into the open cave—a grave of dead men's bones—by friends eager to return to the protection of the city walls as Moabite oppressors approached.

Elisha died, and they buried him. Now the bands of the Moabites would invade the land in the spring of the year. As they were burying a man, behold, they saw a marauding band; and they cast the man into the grave of Elisha. And when the man touched the bones of Elisha he revived and stood up on his feet.[11]

---

9. "Dead Poets Society (1989): Quotes," IMDb.com, accessed March 28, 2018, http://www.imdb.com/title/tt0097165/quotes.

10. 2 Kings 13:14–19.

11. 2 Kings 13:20–21.

This happened in spring, the season of new life. Yet death was evident, with Elisha's bones being all that remained of this son of the tribe of Issachar. His flesh had completely decomposed. Perhaps it was between one and three years since he died; we do not know. Certainly, a body exposed to nature (and apart from wild beasts invading the cave) could thoroughly decompose within three years' time.

In Scripture, bones are a metaphor relating to the promises of God and His destiny for Israel, and ultimately the Church. Scattered bones speak of disconnection and judgment;[12] they signify His people being cut off from one another and from any hope for the future. The Hebrews didn't want their bones scattered. Neither did they want them burned. In Ezekiel's vision, the bones were burned and cursed, and they spoke of promises for their future being broken.[13]

However, Elisha's bones were preserved, connected and intact. So to what do this dead prophet's bones point? The psalmist wrote, "He [Yahweh] keeps all his bones, not one of them is broken." John the Beloved, the only male disciple who did not abandon Jesus at the cross, would remember this. He endured the horrific scene along with Mary, the mother of Jesus; Mary Magdalene; and Mary, the wife of Cleopas. John watched Jesus's sufferings unfold and witnessed the event's climax, about which he offered this insight: "For these things took place that the Scripture might be fulfilled: 'Not one of his bones will be broken.'"[14]

None of Christ's bones were broken or disconnected because none of His promises failed or will ever fail! Elisha, the dead prophet from the sons of Issachar was not intended to have a living successor who had not first died. Instead, Elisha's

12. Ezek. 37.

13. Psalms 34:20.

14. John 19:36 (ESV).

story foreshadowed the reality that resurrection power works best in graveyards!

The spring season was the Passover-First Fruits Season, the foreshadowing of death, burial, and resurrection. So enough with the talk of Elisha's failed succession plan! His story has nothing to do with that and everything to do with God raising up sons and daughters who were dead in their transgressions and sins and made alive in Christ to carry on the prophetic legacy of the sons of Issachar. "For we are parts of his body—of his flesh and of his bones."[15]

Perhaps you are stirred by these thoughts. I pray that you are. As you read the coming pages, I invite you to consider what it means to be part of that company of people who will passionately pursue an extraordinary life in the Spirit and see themselves as part of the Dead Prophets Society.

Dr. Mark Chironna
Holy Week, 2018

---

15. Eph. 5:30 (ISV); see also Gen. 2:23.

INTRODUCTION

The Pharisees and Sadducees came, and to test him they asked him to show them a sign from heaven. He answered them, "When it is evening, you say, 'It will be fair weather, for the sky is red.' And in the morning, 'It will be stormy today, for the sky is red and threatening.' You know how to interpret the appearance of the sky, but you cannot interpret the signs of the times."[1] —Jesus of Nazareth

FOR MILLENNIA, SAILORS HAVE FOLLOWED a simple rule of thumb that was familiar to Jesus of Nazareth: "Red sun at night, sailor's delight. Red sun at morning, sailors take warning!" A rule of thumb is not an ironclad calculation but "a general or approximate principle, procedure, or rule based on experience or practice."[2] This one speaks to the observation and understanding of weather patterns by which seafarers anticipate changes and chart safe passage to desired havens and ports of call.

Rules of thumb may be general or approximate, but they are not one-offs. For untold generations, mariners studied the nuances of sun and sky and, through their experiences, compiled the data. The resulting axiom isn't perfect but when it

---

1. Matt. 16:1–3 (ESV).

2. Dictionary.com, *Dictionary.com Unabridged* (Random House), accessed: February 18, 2017, http://www.dictionary.com/browse/rule-of-thumb.

is applied, sun and sky become "signs of the times" that help mariners form accurate expectations and navigate wisely.

When Jesus shared the mariners' wisdom in Matthew chapter 16, He was not speaking to sailors but to Pharisees. These were the spiritual fathers of ancient Israel and the progenitors of modern Judaism who revered the Torah of Moses and the oral tradition they said arrived with the Ten Commandments. The Jews considered the Pharisees to be the most honorable leaders in the faith and stewards of the oracles of God. Yet when the Oracle Himself became flesh, they rejected and vehemently opposed Him.

Jesus marveled at how easily the Pharisees could read the skies yet fail to discern the signs of their times. History had reached critical mass, a monumental point of convergence that was about to change everything. The Pharisees, however, were blinded by hypocrisy. Because of it, Jesus leveled His most stinging rebukes against them.[3]

Not all Pharisees rejected Jesus. Nicodemus and Joseph of Arimathea secretly believed in Him.[4] Despite their standing in the religious community, they recognized in Jesus something their peers failed to see. Nicodemus and Joseph understood the signs of the times and governed themselves accordingly.

UNDERSTANDING AND GOVERNANCE

Jesus's remarks about interpreting the signs of the times could be a reference, whether veiled or direct, to what the ancient chronicler wrote regarding leaders of another Jewish group, the tribe of Issachar. They were "men who had *understanding of the times*, to know what Israel ought to do, 200 chiefs, and all their kinsmen under their command."[5]

---

3. Matt. 15:1–7, 14; 23:1–5, 13, 25–29.

4. John 3:1–21, 19:38; Mark 15:42–47.

5. 1 Chron. 12:32 (ESV).

These "sons of Issachar"[6] distinguished themselves from the rest of Israel's tribes through their incisive interpretations of current reality. The chronicler's description of them was given in the context of a particular point in Israel's history: the public recognition by leaders that the nation's future belonged to David and not Saul. Israel's governance was shifting, and because the sons of Issachar understood the times, they perceived the shift and knew which actions the nation should take.

Another Bible account reveals a similar dynamic, this time in the context of the Persian kingdom and Queen Vashti's resistance to King Ahasuerus's governance. Intending to deal justly with his queen's offense, Ahasuerus asked for guidance from "the wise men *who knew the times* (for this was the king's procedure toward all who were versed in law and judgment...)."[7]

Vashti failed miserably to understand Persian governance and the signs of the times. But God had His hand on a successor, Esther, a young Jewish woman whose understanding of God and history had been developed over time. Orphaned as a child, she was adopted by her cousin Mordecai, who raised her as his own daughter. When Vashti lost her crown, Esther was prepared to reign in her place. In a moment of convergence that was critical to the Jews' survival, Mordecai confirmed Esther's assignment and urged her to approach the king:

If you keep silent at this time, relief and deliverance will rise for the Jews from another place, but you and your father's house will perish. And who knows whether you have not come to the kingdom for such a time as this?[8]

---

6. As translated in the *New American Standard* version of First Chronicles 12:32.

7. Esther 1:13 (ESV).

8. Esther 4:14 (ESV).

For Esther, obedience meant risking everything for God and His people. She famously replied, "Then I will go to the king, though it is against the law, and if I perish, I perish."[9]

Mordecai's guidance and Esther's actions required an understanding of the times and seasons. They faced the same question David's contemporaries faced: "How are God's people to be governed?"

This question applies in every generation, including the days of Jesus's earthly walk. As the true son of Issachar, Jesus revealed that understanding the times means perceiving the hand of His Father working and shaping the events of history to fulfill His ultimate intention.[10] Based on the New Creation reality established by Jesus's death, burial, resurrection, and ascension, and the outpouring of His Spirit on all flesh, every generation of Christ's followers is empowered to discern the hand of God working and shaping the events of their times.

That ability has to be understood and applied, however. The whole earth is under Christ's governance, and He is ruling the nations even now.[11] Yet how often do we fail to discern what He is doing? How often has the Church mismanaged and misplaced its expectations (much as the Pharisees did) or forgotten its hard-fought, time-tested "rules of thumb" for discerning the signs of the times?

History is instructive, if we will search it out. The following questions are key to grasping the real meaning of the biblical record:

What motivated the Pharisees to oppose Jesus even while His disciples followed Him?

What was Jesus up to and where was He going?

9. Esther 4:16 (ESV).

10. John 5:19–20.

11. Ps. 22:28.

What internal factors and external triggers caused the Pharisees and Jesus's disciples to respond as they did?

How well-versed were the Pharisees in law and custom? And if they were well-versed, how did they misinterpret the times and fail to recognize their Messiah?

How unlearned were the "unlearned fishermen"?[12] *And, if they were unlearned, how did they recognize the Christ when religious leaders missed Him?*

Answering these questions will keep us humble. Jesus did not choose Pharisees to be in His core group. He chose a small number of ordinary people to walk with Him and to change the world He left them. These "unlearned fishermen" gained something as they walked with the greatest Hebrew scholar who ever lived: they learned to understand the times, to know what needed to be done, and to properly govern themselves in fulfillment of God's ultimate intention.

THE "PROPHETHOOD OF ALL BELIEVERS"

Why do ancient examples matter to us? They speak to our need for thought leaders and trendsetters who are "led by the Spirit."[13] These are "go to" experts with a finger on the pulse of where things are, where they have been, and where they can potentially go. They "have a handle" on these matters; it is their leverage and they know how to use it.

Where are these Spirit-led thought leaders and trendsetters who understand the times and the divine plan of governance and recognize the alternative future God desires for the nations? And *who* are they? Is their ability reserved for the select few, as it was when the books of First and Second Chronicles were written? Or have those who are in Christ come into what

---

12. Acts 4:13. In its historical context, the term *unlearned fishermen* was derogatory, being used by elite academic thought leaders of the day.

13. Rom. 8:14.

Pentecostal theologian Roger Stronstad calls "the prophethood of all believers"?[14]

Stronstad argues that the Holy Spirit baptism empowers believers to act prophetically in the midst of a fallen world, so that they might fulfill the gospel mandate. He also argues for local assemblies being prophetic communities, a perspective that resonates with theologian Walter Brueggemann's concept of "alternative communities."[15]

The prophethood of all believers is not a new concept. Its roots are found in the same ancient Torah where a more familiar concept, the priesthood of all believers, was first forecast by Moses:

> *Moses went up to God, and the LORD called to him from the mountain, saying, "Thus you shall say to the house of Jacob and tell the sons of Israel: 'You yourselves have seen what I did to the Egyptians, and how I bore you on eagles' wings, and brought you to Myself. Now then, if you will indeed obey My voice and keep My covenant, then you shall be My own possession among all the peoples, for all the earth is Mine; and you shall be to Me **a kingdom of priests** and a holy nation.' These are the words that you shall speak to the sons of Israel."*[16]

As parts of a single covenant, the Old and New Testaments are fully consistent with one another. Therefore, it is not surprising that our priesthood and prophethood in Christ were foretold in Torah and have been discussed ever since. Our priesthood was a major tenet of the Magisterial Reformers (Calvin, Zwingli, and Luther) and is a broadly settled one. Our prophethood applies to every New Testament believer

---

14. Roger Stronstad, *The Prophethood of All Believers: A Study in Luke's Charismatic Theology* (Cleveland: CPT Press, 2010).

15. Walter Brueggemann, *Testimony to the Otherwise: The Witness of Elijah and Elisha* (St. Louis: Chalice Press, 2002), 5.

16. Exod. 19:3–6.

but does not suggest that all carry the Ephesians 4:11 calling of *prophetes* (the ascension-gifts prophet).[17] The prophet's office is specifically coupled with that of the apostle to ensure the healthy structure and function of the local church.[18] The prophethood of all believers speaks instead to the essential nature of all who are baptized in the Holy Spirit.

This prophethood was foretold in the narrative of Numbers 11. The context was Israel's continual complaining, God's judgment upon them, and Moses's sense of overwhelm with the burden of leading millions of people whose persistent desire to return to Egyptian enslavement eclipsed their ability to lean forward toward the land of abundance.

To lead this difficult nation, God instructed Moses to gather seventy elders at the Tent of Meeting, where God would put His Spirit upon them for service. Sure enough, the men who gathered began to prophesy. So did Eldad and Medad, two men who remained in the camp. Joshua was offended by the unfairness of their prophesying and asked Moses to forbid the non-attenders from participating.

Moses's response hinted at God's ultimate intention. In what was essentially a veiled prayer, Moses asked Joshua, "Are

---

17. Strong's Greek 4396 "*prophḗtēs* (from 4253 /*pró*, 'beforehand' and 5346 /*phēmí*, 'elevating/asserting one idea over another, especially through the spoken-word')—properly, one who *speaks forth* by the inspiration of God; a *prophet*. A prophet (4396 /*prophḗtēs*) declares the mind (message) of God, which sometimes predicts the future (foretelling) – and more commonly, *speaks forth* His message for a particular situation. 4396 /*prophḗtēs* ('a prophet') then is someone inspired by God to *foretell* or *tellforth* (*forthtell*) the Word of God." "4396. prophétes," Bible Hub, accessed January 18, 2018, http://biblehub.com/greek/4396.htm.

18. The Ephesians 4:11 calling specifically relates to the governance of local assemblies; this is distinct from the idea that the local church as a whole or the body of Christ as a whole functions prophetically as an alternative community within the surrounding culture.

you jealous for my sake? Would that *all* the LORD's people were prophets, that the LORD would put his Spirit on them!"[19]

God answered Moses's prayer on the Day of Pentecost.

PREPARE FOR EXODUS

Understanding the times and knowing what to do requires searching the metanarrative of Scripture (the overarching story represented in hundreds of smaller storylines found in the Bible's books, chapters, and passages) and connecting the dots. From beginning to end, from protology to eschatology, and from first mention to last, it is the primary source of hard data that demands and shapes our response.

The pressurized march of unfolding reality tempts us to appraise situations according to the evidence of the moment. However, snapshots cannot produce accurate appraisals. The freeze-frame of *now* is flanked on one end by history and on the other by what is still to come. Understanding the times and seasons requires (at minimum) the ability to recognize historic patterns and the "wild cards" that disrupt them. As George Santayana said: "Those who cannot remember the past are condemned to repeat it." To seize the future or even the moment demands a sound grasp on current reality, the past that shaped it, and the surprises that history warns us to expect.

For followers of Jesus in the postmodern era, these skills remain essential. Great potential and possibility stand alongside the problems and pitfalls of our current reality. Identifying potential in the midst of our problems requires a keen eye and a willingness to examine ourselves and our weaknesses, the roots of which may be buried deep in the soil of Church history, the culture of a denomination, or the subcultures within them. Whatever our ills, subtle deception can trick us into believing that being in Christ inoculates us against the

---

19. Num. 11:29.

grumbling, complaining, and blindness that plagued the wilderness generation and the first-century Pharisees.

The apostle Paul made it clear that no one is immune to deception, so he called us to humbly recognize the patterns that can tell us where we are.[20] Until problems and pitfalls are detected and properly defined, the axe cannot be "laid at the root of the trees"[21] to (1) sever the supply lines that have nourished our disappointing fruit, and (2) prevent it from growing again.

Often, in the epochs and seasons of Church history, it takes an Elijah or John the Baptist[22] to get to these root issues and turn the hearts of the fathers back to the children.[23] The divine intent is not for fathers to recede, but to lean forward into the future, serving and training sons and daughters of the faith to resist the negative patterns of the known past and, instead, shape new and unknown futures.

Breakthroughs of this kind are exodus events. They require preparation and positioning so the people can slough off old ways of *being* and *doing* and embrace new and unfamiliar ones. The God of all exodus events is faithful, making a way out of no way and activating the event through fresh baptismal waters of death and burial that yield hope, a better future, and more—*a resurrection*.

The dynamics that prepare us for exodus are always creative. If God's creative power seems absent, we have probably become too comfortable within the prevailing culture. Instead of embracing the kingdom culture—which is inherently subversive and never subject to earthly modalities—a comfortable

---

20. "Now these things happened to them as an example, but they were written down for our instruction, on whom the end of the ages has come." 1 Cor. 10:11 (ESV).

21. Matt. 3:10.

22. Matt. 11:14.

23. Mal. 4:6.

Church accommodates worldly norms and acclimates itself to them.

An accommodating Church demands little of itself. By contrast, the preparatory dynamics of the Elijah and John the Baptist typology require the rebuilding of altars and the fresh sacrifice of our lives. The Elijah-Elisha transfer we will soon discuss foreshadows the Jesus-and-His-disciples transfer that leads to "greater works"[24] (specifically, the outpouring of the Spirit on the Day of Pentecost, when the disciples of the ascended Christ were "clothed with power from on high.")[25]

Elisha is a key figure in our study. As a true son of Issachar,[26] he lived in Abel-meholah, in Issachar territory.[27] Elijah had to go there to find the rightful heir of his spirit.[28] Immediately, Elisha left his natural father and allowed Elijah to father him in the things of Yahweh. Like his mentor, Elisha learned to use words infused with "prophetic imagination,"[29] words that activated alternative futures, much as John the Baptist and Jesus did centuries later.

From their stories, we can see that imagination and vision are intertwined. For Walter Brueggemann, the imagination is the "liberated capacity to picture (image) reality in alternative ways outside conventional, commonplace accepted givens."[30] To have a voice, God's prophetic community, the Church, must have a vision, which involves imagination. When the Church instead resists Christ's kingdom and accommodates the

---

24. John 14:12.

25. Luke 24:49.

26. Gen. 49:14–15.

27. 1 Kings 19:16.

28. 2 Kings 2:15. Meaning, "the spirit of Elijah."

29. Walter Brueggemann, *The Prophetic Imagination* (Minneapolis: Fortress Press, 1978).

30. Brueggemann, *Testimony to the Otherwise*, 32.

surrounding culture, its prophetic imagination withers and its vision is lost.

Unless the suppressed prophetic imagination is restored to full vigor, it will rob a generation *or generations* of innovation and creativity. It takes someone like Elijah to spark the recovery, not by operating within the culture's comfortable paradigms but by stepping beyond them. This is what John the Baptist did. In true prophetic fashion, he arrived on the scene evoking the style and presence of Elijah and borrowing from the histories of Elijah and Moses (who also spent years in the desert before going public).[31]

Mark describes the appearing of John the Baptist:

John appeared, baptizing in the wilderness and proclaiming a baptism of repentance for the forgiveness of sins. And all the country of Judea and all Jerusalem ***were going out to him*** *and were being baptized by him in the river Jordan confessing their sins. Now John was clothed with camel's hair and wore a leather belt around his waist and ate locusts and wild honey.*[32]

John summoned Israel to the ultimate exodus event,[33] which led to an alternative community established by and in Christ Jesus.[34] Some in John's day accepted the invitation. Many did

---

31. Luke 1:80, 1 Kings 17:1, Exod. 2:15–4:31.

32. Mark 1:4–6.

33. In Luke 9:31, Luke tells us that Moses and Elijah "appeared in glory" to Jesus on the Mount of Transfiguration "and spoke of his departure, which he was about to accomplish at Jerusalem." The word in the Greek for "departure" is *exodos*, which implies and foreshadows Christ's work as the prophet who was like Moses (see Deut. 18:15; Acts 3:22)—the One who would, by the cross, deliver us from sin as Moses delivered Israel from Pharaoh, and "make a way out of no way" by the parting of the waters.

34. Brueggemann speaks of summoning and nurturing "an alternative community with an alternative identity, vision, and vocation, preoccupied with praise and obedience toward the God we Christians know fully in Jesus of Nazareth." *Testimony to the Otherwise,* 5.

not, including many leaders of the Jews. How easily our human frailty can keep us out of sync, out of step, out of touch, and out of sorts when unexpected events usher us from one paradigm to another!

Paradigm shifting requires flexibility and adaptability.[35] In the late 1960s, a musical group known as The Chicago Transit Authority shifted settled paradigms of genre by blending big-band-era brass sounds with the heart of rock and roll. The group's approach blurred the lines and stretched contemporary musical understanding with a clear, distinct sound—the sound of Lee Loughnane's trumpet. For some, it was too strange a sound to be welcomed, but for those who perceived the shift, it called forth something fresh and alive.

When it comes to walking in the Spirit, there is a parallel, prophetically speaking, by which a distinct sound produces a shift. The apostle Paul described it when he asked, "If the trumpet doesn't sound a clear call, who will get ready for battle?"[36] Such a sound was heard in Paul's own lifetime. It was the voice of Jesus, which was "like the sound of a trumpet."[37] He called the troops into position, saying, "The time is fulfilled, and the kingdom of God is at hand; repent and believe in the gospel."[38]

THE POWER OF STORY

At some point, all human beings become curious about the future. The reason is both simple and practical: the more we know about what is ahead, the better we can prepare for it. We

---

35. Paradigm shifting requires flexibility and adaptability. Thomas S. Kuhn coined the term *paradigm shift*. It refers to changes that occur when existing assumptions and approaches (paradigms) no longer suffice, making a shift necessary. Thomas S. Kuhn, *The Structure of Scientific Revolutions* (Chicago: University of Chicago Press, 1962).

36. 1 Cor. 14:8 (GW).

37. Rev. 1:10.

38. Mark 1:15.

like being prepared because we like being in control. Crossing the threshold from a known chapter into a new and unknown one produces the opposite of control, which is uncertainty. So we look for clues to help us manage it.

The challenge is that our way of seeing can negatively impact our ability to manage life's unfolding. In her landmark work, *Wired for Story*, Lisa Cron explains that our neurological wiring causes us to "see the world not as it is, but as we believe it to be."[39] Unconsciously, we generate self-fulfilling prophecies because we experience what we *believe* is true, whether it is true or not. We also exclude portions of reality that we need to see but choose to deny.

Our penchant for this is greater than we realize. We are incredibly adept at self-deception and very capable of being misled. This is why conspiracy theories are so infectious. Our best defense against such deceptions is to own our susceptibility, in part by recognizing the prejudgments that distort our beliefs, damage our decision-making, and short-circuit the critical thinking and analytical reasoning that move us toward wholeness and well-being.

Our desire for foresight is natural and inherently human; but without the hard data gleaned from clear hindsight, it can be wildly inaccurate. It is impossible to illuminate our current reality (no less the future) without an accurate, objective appraisal of the past and the choices that have largely shaped our current state. We know that repeating those choices will produce more of the same. However, when insight and hindsight are aligned with the truth, foresight becomes more sound and a healthier future can emerge.

It bears repeating that those who are in Christ *can be* deceived. Even in Pentecostal and Charismatic circles where

---

39. Lisa Cron, "Digging Up Your Protagonist's Inner Issue," in *Wired for Story: The Writer's Guide to Using Brain Science to Hook Readers from the Very First Sentence* (New York: Ten Speed Press, 2012), 84.

the freedom of the Spirit is emphasized, many ignore Paul's warning to the Corinthians: "We know in part and we prophesy in part."[40] Many who claim they have "revelation" from God forget how limited *gnosis* (knowledge that comes through personal experience) is. Revelation is frequently claimed and then pronounced without accountability. Scriptural authority, the authority of the Spirit who inspired the Scriptures, the clear teachings of Jesus, and the biblical authority of the local and historical Church are set aside as though revelation were infallible and prophecy were equal with Scripture itself.

What a dangerous supposition this is! Granted, it is often unintended. If questioned, most errant "prophets" would deny supporting it. In practice, however, to declare one's "revelation" and then teach it without scrutiny and oversight, is to equate it with scriptural authority, or at least consider it equal in authority to the declarations of the Old Testament prophets.

This approach is not only disconcerting but discrediting. It is one of the main reasons Cessationists take issue with Continuationists. Paul, a scholar's scholar, would also take issue with it. Today, however, untaught, unprincipled, and unstable believers still distort Paul's counsel,[41] abuse their callings, and even ignore his clear admonitions to the church at Corinth.

This ought not to be. Seeing the gravity of the situation in his own day and the potential for future abuses, Paul pulled rank on ungrounded voices and codified his warnings in his letters. Through them, he invites us to yield to the apostolic authority, gnosis, and wisdom behind this sobering statement: "If anyone thinks that he is a prophet, or spiritual, he should acknowledge that the things I am writing to you are a command of the Lord."[42]

---

40. 1 Cor. 13:9.

41. 2 Pet. 3:16.

42. 1 Cor. 14:37 (ESV).

This is part of our story. In the chapters that follow, we will examine these and other issues. Paul's guidance will underlie the conversation, not to dampen the charismatic spirit but to build it up and the Church with it. We will search the heart of God and the hard data of Scripture and biblical history with an eye toward discovering (1) what wants to happen in His eternal purposes, and (2) what kind of company we are called to be.

In seeking to understand the times and to know what we should do, we will consider

- the signs of our times and historical parallels; shakings and the unshakeable kingdom;

- the nature, calling, and history of the sons of Issachar and the implications for the twenty-first century;

- biblical distinctions between *time* and *times*; what the future is and isn't, historical "wild cards," and the importance of alternative futures to the prevailing culture;

- the typology of the Elijah-Elisha narrative: its relevance to the sons of Issachar and the implications of the transferred mantle, the shift, the double portion, and alternative futures;

- the ascended Christ and His Church, the Trinity as the foundation for all revelation, the invisible realm as the "real world," the sanctified imagination, an open versus a closed system, and alternative futures;

- the anointing that flows from Jesus, the Head, to His body, the double portion as the promised "greater works," Elisha's trusting of the mantle, embracing our priesthood, and the heavenly council and its members;

- the Church as God's instrument of recovery, its need for and role in restoration and the rebuilding of kingdom culture, the power of spiritual sight, the believer's authority and membership in the council of God.

THE DEAD PROPHETS SOCIETY

As you journey through these pages, may your sense of calling find its ultimate expression in your expanded understanding of the times.

CHAPTER 1

OFF THE FENCE AND ON THE LIVING EDGE

THE WORLD IS IN TUMULT. Precipitous change has become the norm, and is becoming more "normal" every day.[1] The tectonic plates of world culture are shifting and fault lines are hardening. Political correctness has polarized and paralyzed discourse. Common sense is equated with ignorance. Wickedness holds court in high places. The ungodly pontificate to the masses. They mock God, persecute His people, and ignore His voice.

Such phenomena are not new. The books of First and Second Kings reveal Israel's desire to be like other nations. It records the syncretistic compromises and shocking failures of Israel's kings to heed God's prophets. Although a few kings honored the prophets and experienced Yahweh's good intentions for their

---

1. According to Richard Paul, "New global realities are rapidly working their way into the deepest structures of our lives: economic, social, environmental realities—realities with profound implications for teaching and learning, for business and politics, for human rights and human conflicts." Richard Paul, "Accelerating Change," The Critical Thinking Community, accessed January 7, 2017, http://www.criticalthinking.org/pages/accelerating-change/474. Content reprised from Richard Paul, *Critical Thinking: How to Prepare Students for a Rapidly Changing World*, eds. Jane Willsen and A. J. A. Binker (Santa Rosa, CA: Foundation for Critical Thinking, 1995), 1.

nation, many killed the prophets and were judged.[2] Even *The Prophet*, Jesus Christ, was delivered up to an oppressive government to die an undignified and shameful death.

With the backdrop of history in mind, the world's fallen condition comes as no shock. Instead, the blow is that much of Christ's Church has also abandoned the way, the truth, and the life. In some quarters, the new wine has been drained to the dregs. Where the life of the Spirit once thrived, the traditions of men have taken hold, as though Jesus and Paul had never warned against them.[3] Holiness is often reduced to proscriptions about smoking, drinking, and sex, or cast off as an Old Testament vestige. "Enlightened" academic arguments rail against eternal truths. Even Christ's divinity is challenged in, of all places, Evangelicalism.

The Church is being tried. The same political correctness that poisons the culture also silences Christian voices. In all settings, leaders and others "feel inhibited and afraid to address even the most banal issues directly."[4] When controversies arise, some shepherds turn their pulpits and pews into "safe spaces" from which they nurse the sensitivities of those who find God's commands inconvenient or in conflict with their personal and cultural preferences. Instead of laying down their lives for the sheep, leaders become hired hands preaching sanitized, "inclusive" messages that offend no one except lovers of the truth.[5] Their precautions are meant to promote unity, but they foment division, which keeps the Church from multiplying.

---

2. Matt. 23:37.

3. Mark 7:8; Col. 2:8.

4. Robin J. Ely, Debra Meyerson, and Martin N. Davidson, "Rethinking Political Correctness," *Harvard Business Review* (September 2006), accessed January 7, 2017, https://hbr.org/2006/09/rethinking-political-correctness.

5. John 10:11–13.

This is the tepid climate in which believers become fence-sitters. Removed from the living edge of the faith, they lose sight of the cultural fault lines that are now the frontlines of the gospel they profess. Meanwhile, those leaders who shrink back from the fray focus instead on church growth and program expansion. They give lip service to the gospel, but do not incarnate Christ in the culture. These realities are more than empirical facts. They are signs pointing to where we are and where we are going. At first glance, the picture seems entirely diabolical. But looks are deceiving. If we learn to read the signs accurately and move beyond our fear, we will see where death is being swallowed up in life.

Signs are important, but so are *the times*. Five hundred years after the Great Reformation, a great restoration is unfolding, and with it, a critical resurgence of prophetic function. Instead of leaders whose celebrity and titles go before them to mesmerize audiences, we need leaders who are impressed with the name of Jesus Christ only, a people who can acknowledge the shaking all around them and in their own lives, without being shaken from the faith or their belief in a sovereign God.

Is God drawing such leaders to become a sold-out company that discerns the times and loves laboring in the kingdom? Are modern-day Elishas in their ranks?

Such a company—a remnant of twenty-first-century sons and daughters of Issachar who live to carry the burden of the Lord—may already be stirring among those who see beyond the circumstantial and into the sacred. Regardless of the cultural climate, the state of the Church, or the cost of their callings, they would be a people devoted and alert to God's eternal purpose. And when the world around them quakes, they would know what it means and what they must do.

THE SHAKING AND THE UNSHAKABLE KINGDOM

You don't have to be a prophet to sense that everything that can be shaken *is being shaken*. A level of acuity is needed, however, to interpret the nature and purpose of the shaking. To begin with, we need to be aware that "tabloid prophecies," which promote a sensationalized theology based in current events, are less about the truth and more about our penchant for conspiracy theories. Doom and gloom mythologies sell books, but do they honor the ascended Christ?

Haggai and other prophets point us to true north and empower us to reclaim our rightful future by explaining what the shaking actually means. First, their writings prove that generations before us have been shaken. Like them, our response begins with our theology, which can only be sound if our understanding, observations, and interpretations of the shaking are biblical. Until and unless we perceive events according to the hard data revealed in Scripture, we will not receive all that God has prepared for us.

With the threefold cord of the Son, the Spirit, and the Scriptures as our beginning and endpoint,[6] we find a clue that Haggai hid in plain sight:

> For thus says the LORD of hosts, "Once more in a little while, I am going to shake the heavens and the earth, the sea also and the dry land. I will shake all the nations; and they will come with the wealth of all nations, and I will fill this house with glory," says the LORD of hosts.[7]

Many contemporary theories have been floated in regard to the shaking now underway. But are they aligned with Scripture? Inspired by the Holy Spirit, Haggai named the source of the shaking: it is God Himself. Satan would love to claim

---

6. Leonard Sweet, "DMIN Applied Semiotics and Future Leadership Studies" (lectures, George Fox University, Portland, Oregon, October 13, 2014). Dr. Sweet speaks metaphorically of a "holy braid" of "the Son, the Spirit, the Scriptures" that cannot be separated. He explains that "if they are twined together and twisted tight, there is nothing stronger...no rope can carry more weight...but if they become separated and untwined, the whole shebang falls apart."

7. Hag. 2:6–7.

credit for the current chaos, but the shaking is not his doing. It is God's. Therefore, we can be sure it serves the divine intent. God knows exactly what the shaking will produce and how it will serve His eternal purpose.

God's determined will is confirmed by the writer to the Hebrews, who connects the shaking to His voice:

See to it that you do not refuse Him who is speaking. For if those did not escape when they refused him who warned them on earth, much less will we escape who turn away from Him who warns from heaven. And His voice shook the earth then, but now He has promised, saying, "YET ONCE MORE I WILL SHAKE NOT ONLY THE EARTH, BUT ALSO THE HEAVEN."[8]

God honors His promises. If He says He will shake the realms, He will! And regardless of our discomfort, it will reflect His love. In the passage from Haggai 2, the Hebrew word for "shake" is *ra`ash*, which speaks of shaking, quaking, and causing to quake. But the word has another, more unexpected aspect: it means "to cause to spring or leap."[9] So, instead of pulling everything down, *ra`ash* creates forward motion—the kind of vigorous leap a horse makes when it vaults ahead on all fours.

God's shaking is not a death knell, but a great leap forward!

Hebrews 12:27 increases our understanding by explaining what the shaking is designed to do. It says, "'Yet once more,' denotes the *removing* of those things which can be shaken."[10]

The word *removing* sounds negative, because we naturally equate removal with subtraction. But the original Greek

---

8. Heb. 12:25–26.

9. *Strong's Hebrew Lexicon*, Blue Letter Bible, s.v. "ra`ash" (Strong's H7493), accessed January 5, 2017, https://www.blueletterbible.org//lang/lexicon/lexicon.cfm?Strongs=H7493&t=NASB. The word also suggests the leaping of a locust or grasshopper. These creatures spring great distances, relative to their size.

10. Heb. 12:27.

word *metathesis* says more. It does describe the transferring or translating of something "from one place to another,"[11] but it also speaks of change. So, God's shaking is not a minus; it's a transformation!

Metathesis is used elsewhere, including to describe the great leap from the Aaronic order to the order of Melchizedek. It was a seismic, transformational shift by which Jesus Christ replaced the Aaronic priesthood and became our Great High Priest.[12] To many first-century Jews, this was a threatening proposition. But to the lost and all who long to be restored, it makes the leap from death to life possible.

Scripture is packed full of divine leaps. The writer to the Hebrews noted one in which Enoch was "taken up" to heaven.[13] Here the Holy Spirit chose a similar word, *metatithēmi*, from the same root as *metathesis*. It conveys the idea that Enoch was transposed or transferred (i.e., "translated" from one realm to another). Not surprisingly, *metatithēmi* also means "to change."[14]

Word choices in Scripture are precise and also revelatory, but only when they are understood. When we dig into the original languages, we uncover the powerful images hidden for us by the Holy Spirit. Some of those images have already clarified God's intent where the divine shaking is concerned. This clarity positions us to experience and interpret the shaking accurately, so that instead of fear and confusion, we anticipate forward motion and transformation. That is *revelation*.

11. *Strong's Greek Lexicon,* Blue Letter Bible, s.v. "metathesis" (Strong's G3331), accessed January 5, 2017, https://www.blueletterbible.org//lang/lexicon/lexicon.cfm?Strongs=G3331&t=NASB.

12. Heb. 7:12.

13. Heb. 11:5.

14. *Strong's Greek Lexicon,* Blue Letter Bible, s.v. "metatithēmi" (Strong's G3346), accessed January 5, 2017, https://www.blueletterbible.org//lang/lexicon/lexicon.cfm?Strongs=G3346&t=NASB.

In regard to the nature of the shaking, an additional clue begins where we left off earlier in Hebrews chapter 12:

*This expression, "Yet once more," denotes the removing of those things which can be shaken, **as of created things**, so that those things which cannot be shaken may remain. Therefore, since we receive **a kingdom which cannot be shaken**, let us show gratitude, by which we may offer to God an acceptable service with reverence and awe; for our God is a consuming fire.*[15]

Not everything can be shaken, but everything that can be, will be. It behooves us to know which things are which. The key lies in the meaning of the term *created things*. The writer to the Hebrews said these things were destined to be shaken. But what exactly are they? Some scholars believe the term refers to the created order. Others interpret it as works of the flesh, which are inherently inferior to anything God creates. Is it possible that "created things" include anything that results from human contrivance?

Consider, for example, the human tendency to create personal "kingdoms." We decide what we want—money, career, power, prestige, the right house, the perfect mate—and we start building. But are our pursuits inspired by the Father's will? Or are we building just to satisfy unmet emotional needs? The former is kingdom; the latter is human contrivance. Solomon warned about this, writing, "Unless the LORD builds the house, they labor in vain who build it; unless the LORD guards the city, the watchman keeps awake in vain."[16]

A SHAKING IN ANCIENT ISRAEL

Kingdoms built on human contrivance are doomed. No matter how high we build our walls and towers, they will be affect-

---

15. Heb. 12:27–29.

16. Ps. 127:1.

ed by the shaking. Just ask Israel. In their history they experienced many shakings, including the demise of King Saul.

It started with Israel's misguided desire to be like neighboring nations, all of which had kings. God intended to give Israel a king at some point, but it would be *His* king in *His* timing. Israel was not content to wait, however. So they pressured the prophet Samuel to get them a king, not on God's terms, but theirs. Samuel understood the folly of their ways and pushed back against their demands. When he asked God what he should do, God essentially said, "Give them what they want."[17]

So Samuel took a vial of oil and anointed Saul, a Benjamite, as Israel's first earthly king. Outwardly, Saul looked the part. He was a handsome man who stood head and shoulders above everyone else. Dazzled by his appearance, the people were sure that Saul would make Israel the envy of the world.

God was not as easily impressed. He never intended Israel to operate on worldly standards or compete on worldly terms. Had Israel perceived and honored His intent, they would have waited and would have spared themselves the fallout Saul's reign ultimately produced. They would have realized that this "ideal" king was a man of low character who was ruled by his insecurities and gnawing fears. His thoughts were corrupted, yet he chose them over what God said. He could be called a "head-and-shoulders king": wherever his head went, his shoulders followed. Had he been teachable, he might have become a worthy king. But he refused God's guidance and continued on the path of human contrivance.

God had to respond. There *had* to be a leap forward.

PEOPLE OF THE LEAP

The last straw in Saul's reign came when he refused to exterminate the Amalekites and destroy all their property as God commanded. The leap had begun: God tore the kingdom from

---

17. 1 Sam. 8:7–8.

him and gave it to someone the people would never have chosen. He gave it to the shepherd boy, David.[18]

When Samuel anointed David, he looked nothing like a king. He was the youngest son of Jesse, a shepherd boy who worshipped God in the pasturelands. The original Hebrew for "youngest" reveals that Jesse saw David as "insignificant... lesser...of low status."[19] His only fighting experience was not against rival kings, but lions and bears. His weapons were not sword and shield, but a sling and a stone. Yet, he was a man after God's own heart.[20] This was the kind of king God was after.

Years after Samuel anointed David, Saul still held power. The leap, however, was irrevocable. Saul knew it and hated David, hunting him down relentlessly, and forcing him to live as an exile.

Thousands of Israelites supported David. Among them was a tribe that immersed itself in the hard data of God's promises and Israel's history. These were not people who hoped for the best or were blown by "every wind of doctrine."[21] They were not fooled by fakes or dazzled by tabloid prophecies. Instead, they were keen observers who accurately interpreted centuries' worth of spiritual data. As a result, they recognized and aligned themselves with the leap God ordained.

These were "the sons of Issachar, men who understood the times, with knowledge of what Israel should do."[22] They understood God's promises and perceived how they spoke to current conditions. The sons of Issachar interpreted events from His perspective, and they trusted His intent and timing. They

---

18. 1 Sam. 15:28.

19. James Swanson, *Dictionary of Biblical Languages with Semantic Domains: Hebrew (Old Testament)*, s.v. "qatan" (Oak Harbor: Logos Research Systems, Inc., 1997).

20. Acts 13:22.

21. Eph. 4:14.

22. 1 Chron. 12:32.

were so well versed in Israel's history with God that they could reach back into the past and summon that which spoke to their future. Therefore, the shaking of Saul's kingdom did not rattle them. They perceived the transformation it portended. Like David, they had God's heart and longed to be part of what He was doing.

It would seem that God seeks such a people today, with traits resembling those of the sons of Issachar: Amid rampant confusion and chaos, they would perceive the leaps ahead. In a darkening world, they would not retreat, but advance. Like the prophet Daniel, they would look up to read the symbols, signs, and night visions God provides. They would know when a shift was coming and would anticipate the opening of portals into new dimensions. Such a company would see the choices God's people face and understand the world's way of seeing. As a people whose prophetic paradigm is shaped by the radical hope of the gospel, they would reject conspiracy theories, sensationalism, and fear-mongers.

Is there such a company? Do they actually believe that the "kingdom of the world has become the kingdom of our Lord and of His Christ"?[23] Will they stand on the living edge of what God is doing and ask

What is Jesus doing?

Where is Jesus going?

Are we going with Him?

What are the signs of our times?

To those who believe the answer is "Yes," the culture's jagged fault lines are the frontlines of their obedience. Though uncertainty and resistance are inevitable, there are willing burden-bearers ready to shoulder the load. Like David, whom Michal mocked for dancing before the Ark in an "undignified"

---

23. Rev. 11:15.

manner, such modern-day sons and daughters of Issachar would gladly become fools for God.

Such a people could indeed be—as J. Ern Baxter was fond of saying during a former visitation—God's vanguard "company." Are we among them? Will we venture onto the living edge that is "Issachar territory"?

WHAT THIS MEANS

If such a company were formed, it would function in realms of high adventure and prophetic insight, not ignoring or denying harsh realities, but seeing them in the light of the gospel and Christ's eternal rule.

The world *is* in crisis and seems to be collapsing under its own weight. Some geopolitical and societal problems are unsolvable. No human agency can strike a perfect balance between preserving civil liberties and defending against terrorist threats, for example. Nor can any diplomat or international body resolve the turmoil in the Middle East. In Syria, hundreds of thousands have perished and more have been displaced. These matters defy earthly solutions. Nevertheless, we can have more faith in the dreams of the Spirit to renew our planet than in the dreams of terrorists and others to destroy it.

The Church has her own crises, including those mentioned earlier. But the Church has been here before. Shakings throughout her history have not destroyed the Church; they have renewed her and propelled her forward. The same holds true today: The testimony of Jesus *will be* recovered. The present and future belong to the saints who belong to Christ, as the apostle Paul explained:

Let no one boast in men. For all things belong to you, whether Paul or Apollos or Cephas or the world or life or death or things present or things to come; all things belong to you, and you belong to Christ; and Christ belongs to God.[24]

---

24. 1 Cor. 3:21–23.

For a vanguard company, the times and leaps will become evident. Whatever our calling, we know this: We are not serving wicked kings, but the King of kings who fulfills all types and shadows of Old Covenant Israel. His coronation did not come by earthly decree, but through His resurrection and ascension. Therefore, His way of conquering the world's kingdoms is also revolutionary. He doesn't do it through an iron fist or a velvet glove; He does it through His faithful witnesses—the kingly priesthood and holy nation, the Church.

Jesus's cross-shaped life and death modeled the cruciform life that is our calling. Like Him, we do not overcome imperial powers through earthly means. Instead, we embody His "revolutionary way of being revolutionary."[25] Whether the world receives or rejects us will hold little weight if we are incarnating His way of being and doing, for His sake and theirs.

Given the division that exists in the Church politically, racially, ideologically, and otherwise, learning how to intentionally and fervently "preserve the unity of the Spirit in the bond of peace,"[26] is essential for every believer. Misunderstanding and division only draw the Church off course. The opportunity is ripe to address these issues head-on and advance the true cause and message of Christ. Then and only then will the world believe the larger truth: that because of His love, the Father sent Jesus to redeem them and fulfill every jot and tittle of Scripture's grand narrative.[27]

---

25. N. T. Wright, *Jesus and the Victory of God: Christian Origins and the Question of God* (Minneapolis: Fortress Press, 1996) 2:564.

26. Eph. 4:3.

27. John 3:16, 17:23.

CHAPTER 2

THE ISSACHAR PROFILE

I F AN ISSACHAR COMPANY EXISTED, what would its characteristics be? The only viable reference point is the biblical record. Issachar's legacy began when Jacob neared his last breath and told his twelve sons, "Assemble yourselves that I may tell you what will befall you in the days to come."[1] With no coddling or mincing of words, Jacob prophesied over each son and over the tribes they were becoming. When he got to Issachar, he issued a blessing that might be mistaken for a curse:

Issachar is a strong donkey, lying down between the sheepfolds. When he saw that a resting place was good and that the land was pleasant, he bowed his shoulder to bear burdens, and became a slave at forced labor.[2]

Donkey references aside, remember that Jacob did not know which territory Issachar would ultimately be assigned. Yet he perceived that it would be a good land, and he was right. Issachar's allotment included the Jezreel valley and was the

---

1. Gen. 49:1.
2. Gen. 49:14–15.

most desirable terrain of all, being well-watered, fertile, and suitable for agriculture and grazing.[3]

Jacob also indicated that Issachar valued the blessing and honored its promise and potential. They knew a good thing when they saw it; they also knew that to realize its fulfillment they would have to own it. That meant working the land and bowing their shoulders to bear whatever burden the calling required. The follow-through would demand character, and the sons of Issachar had it. Hard work was not a curse in their eyes; it was an opportunity to serve the divine purpose.

The tribe's service took many forms. Jacob called them a strong donkey "lying down between the sheepfolds." Most people would flinch from any comparison to an animal known for its stubbornness. Donkeys are strong-willed, independent creatures that do not bond easily. But when a donkey connects with the shepherd, the bond is strong. Nestled among the master's sheep, the donkey protects them from harm and danger. When predators come prowling, the creature that normally calms the flock now becomes its fierce defender, braying loudly to rouse it and its shepherd. If an intruder penetrates, the donkey pounces repeatedly to crush its skull, defending to the death, if necessary.

Issachar is not just *a* donkey; it is Judah's choice donkey jealously guarding the sheep of God's pasture. Unconcerned with personal aggrandizement, Issachar's guiding question is "What's in it for my Master?" Literally and figuratively, Issachar bears his Master and His Master's burdens, even carrying the King in the glorious procession Zechariah prophesied and Matthew confirmed:

Rejoice greatly, O daughter of Zion! Shout in triumph, O daughter of Jerusalem! Behold, your king is coming to you;

---

3. Josh. 19:17–23.

He is just and endowed with salvation, humble, and mounted on a donkey, even on a colt, the foal of a donkey.[4]

SAY TO THE DAUGHTER OF ZION, "BEHOLD YOUR KING IS COMING TO YOU, GENTLE, AND MOUNTED ON A DONKEY, EVEN ON A COLT, THE FOAL OF *A BEAST OF BURDEN.*"[5]

Notice that Matthew mentions "a beast of burden." The ultimate expression of Issachar's role as burden-bearer was to carry the Ark, which is Christ, not grudgingly, but as a love-slave bonded to his Master.

THE ISSACHAR SKILL SET

The divine burden shouldered by the sons of Issachar was not shared through osmosis but by intent. Just as the tribe was diligent to cultivate their land, they also cultivated their understanding of the times, the whole of Torah, and Israel's history with God. According to rabbinic tradition, this working tribe had a scholarly bent, being well versed in the hard data relevant to their calling.

The sons of Issachar were also skilled astronomers[6] who studied and interpreted the movements in the heavens as they related to the seasons and cycles of God's intention.[7] Remember that God said, "Let there be lights in the expanse of the heavens *to separate the day from the night, and let them be for signs and for seasons and for days and years.*"[8] The majestic heavens had a very practical side in God's creative scheme,

4. Zech. 9:9.

5. Matt. 21:5.

6. Robert Jamieson, A. R. Fausset, and David Brown, *Commentary Critical and Explanatory on the Whole Bible*, vol. 1 (Oak Harbor, WA: Logos Research Systems, Inc., 1997), 256.

7. "These men of Issachar were not dull and narrow 'bony asses' (Gen. 49:14), but prudent 'judges of the signs of their time' (Matt. 16:3)." John Peter Lange et al., *A Commentary on the Holy Scriptures: 1 & 2 Chronicles* (Bellingham, WA: Logos Bible Software, 2008), 106.

8. Gen. 1:14.

providing signs that marked day and night and divided one season from another. Decoding the correlations between heavenly movements and the earthly experience of time took centuries of human observation and documentation, which continues to this day.

All of these disciplines were part of Issachar's handling of hard data, which positioned the tribe to discern divine leaps such as the one from the reign of Saul to that of David. That pivot point was the context within which Scripture called them "men who understood the times, with knowledge of what Israel should do."[9] The tribe that loved study and hard work had become a seasoned tribe of leaders bearing sound guidance for the sheep. Their counsel was part and parcel of Issachar's protective role as Judah's donkey.

Issachar's diligence was integral to their leadership role, but their proficiency was not entirely their own doing. The tribe's prophetic paradigm originated with Jacob's proclamation and the laying on of his hands in Genesis chapter 49. In that moment, Jacob imparted to Issachar the prophetic legacy for which the tribe would be known—a legacy they continued to develop through centuries of observation, application, and study.

When we connect the dots in the biblical metanarrative we discover that Issachar's prophetic role was linked to governance. For example, Isaiah prophesied that the government would rest on Messiah's shoulders.[10] Metaphorically speaking, shoulders are tied to governance. We also know that Issachar "bowed his shoulder to bear burdens," and a donkey carried into Jerusalem the Messiah who came as the Incarnation of God's person and intent. Add to this the idea that Judah's choice donkey carries the precious cargo of that

---

9. 1 Chron. 12:32.

10. Isa. 9:6.

which is on God's heart. Bearing God's burdens is clearly linked to the upholding of His government.

As God's burden-bearers, the sons of Issachar became increasingly tuned to His desires. When events or actions testified to God's eternal scheme, the sons of Issachar knew it. And when something opposed God's plan, they discerned that too. When the shift in Israel's governance was on, they recognized David as God's choice and understood why the scepter *had to* leave Saul's hands.

The sons of Issachar discerned these things not as religious nitpickers but as a people who readily separated the genuine from the counterfeit. They knew Saul's motives were "off." He was not a man burdened by what burdened God; he was a man of the flesh driven by his own lusts and greed. Issachar's immersion in Torah and in God's history with Israel informed their understanding of how kings should and should not govern. Regardless of the people's blinding infatuation with Saul, the sons of Issachar saw him as he really was.

Saul did not share in Issachar's understanding. His reign had not pleased God or served the good of Israel. He was not a giver, but a taker. He had not carried himself as a servant-leader but a leader over servants. Therefore, the sons of Issachar were not surprised or offended when the mantle of governance shifted away from him. Nor were they confused about what Israel must do. As burden-bearers devoted to whatever was on God's heart, they anticipated where He was going and pointed Israel in that direction. Their alignment with King David was not a political maneuver; it was an outgrowth of their alignment with God.

Saul was not alone in his lack of understanding. Much of Israel lacked the insights that Issachar had cultivated. Remember that only Samuel, David, and David's family had witnessed David's private anointing years earlier. Most of the people who supported Saul as king knew little or nothing about his disobedience to God or his refusal to repent. They only knew what kind of image they wanted Saul to project to surrounding nations. So, instead of carrying the burden of God's desire for a set-apart people and a king after His own heart, Israel insisted on blending in with their neighbors and elevating their "trophy king."

The sons of Issachar saw the error of Israel's ways. Their two hundred chiefs resisted the culture and set the momentum in favor of God's mandated shift. Remember that Issachar did not shrink back from hard work, but willingly bowed its shoulder to bear the burdens necessary to maintain their assigned territory. Having embraced the blessing declared by their father Jacob centuries earlier, they now continued to embrace the price of its fulfillment. They anticipated the future that wanted to happen and they took their place in leading Israel in the direction of God's eternal purpose.

The sons of Issachar were not completely alone in supporting David. Neither were the people alone in discounting him. Even Samuel, the godly and powerful judge who had anointed Saul, almost missed God's appointed shift. When God took Samuel into His confidence and expressed His regret for ever having anointed Saul, Samuel took it hard and made it personal. God had to shake him from his disillusionment with a pointed question: "How long will you grieve over Saul?"[11]

The question and God's further instruction snapped Samuel out of his paralysis, but even after arriving at Jesse's house, he wavered in the mission and wondered where God was going. His confusion almost ended in the anointing of another "head and shoulders king"! After suffering through the debacle of Saul's failures and of Israel's misguided approach to the throne, Samuel was still tempted by outward appearances to anoint one of the seven sons of Jesse who most looked the part. Had God not opened Samuel's eyes, he would have

---

11. 1 Sam. 16:1.

recreated the known (and miserably unsuccessful) past by replacing Saul with a man just like him.

God, however, was finished with Saul's ilk and directed Samuel to facilitate a new and previously unknown future. The anointing of David was meant to be a game-changer, a *kairos* moment in which God's promise would begin to release the potential it contained. In the natural realm, the process would take time to unfold. Saul's decline and David's succession to the throne took years to complete—years of shaking, danger, and discomfort. But in the fullness of time, God's will was accomplished. Saul was swept from the stage and King David was crowned.

When the transition was ripe, the sons of Issachar were ready. The shaking and uncertainty had not disoriented them. They took events in stride and continued to flow with God. Instead of clinging to the known past, they cleaved to the unexpected future God revealed to them. They were well versed in the lesson Samuel had learned in his near panic at Jesse's house. They had already shaken themselves loose from what heaven had shaken off, and they bound themselves to what was bound to God's eternal purpose.

The times had changed, and Issachar knew it.

FLASK OR HORN?

Two different Hebrew words name the vessels Samuel used to anoint Saul and David. In Saul's case, Samuel poured out the contents of a "vial" or "flask" of oil.[12] The same Hebrew word is used in Second Kings 9 to describe "a small container of perfumed oil,"[13] most likely a man-made vessel. In David's case, however, Samuel anointed

---

12. 1 Sam. 10:1 KJV and NASB, respectively.

13. Chad Brand et al., eds., "Flask," *Holman Illustrated Bible Dictionary* (Nashville, TN: Holman Bible Publishers, 2003), 579.

THE DEAD PROPHETS SOCIETY

him with a horn of oil, which is a God-made vessel (i.e., a ram's horn). The horn's capacity far exceeds that of a vial, and because the horn comes from an animal, blood must be spilled before it can be used as a container.

The difference in vessels is meaningful. Man-made vessels are a metaphor for human frailty, but a horn speaks of strength and authority.[14] The shedding of blood to create the horn reminds us that before we can be anointed, we must come under the blood of the Lamb.

The choice of vessels seems to highlight the differences between Saul and David. The first man had a frail character, a small capacity for God's anointing, and was "man-made" rather than God-chosen. The second was a man after God's own heart, soaked in His anointing and hand-picked by Him.

THE "NO" TEST

Samuel was not a flawless man, but he was a stalwart prophet. His struggle with Saul's demise and David's appointment to the throne does not suggest that Samuel was in any way disqualified for his calling. What the story illustrates is the very human and often messy context within which we serve God. The bewildering process that led to Samuel's "discovery" of David was not quite a textbook example of how to anoint a king. But that might be precisely the point. The leap from Saul to David was not meant to fit a mold. It was meant to break one.

Remember that Samuel endured a nerve-wracking and probably embarrassing test as he worked through David's seven brothers. It was arguably the toughest kind of test God's

---

14. *Strong's Hebrew Lexicon*, Blue Letter Bible, s.v. "qeren" (Strong's H7161), accessed February 3, 2017, https://www.blueletterbible.org// lang/lexicon/lexicon.cfm?Strongs=H7161&t=KJV. This word can also indicate a flask, but the fact that a word different from that used in 1 Samuel 10:1, would indicate "horn" as the intention.

50

people face: God's firm, unwavering *no*. As Samuel considered each candidate, that was all he got: "No. No. No. No. No. No. No."

No doubt, the accuser whispered to Samuel, "You're on a fool's errand."

Anybody in Samuel's shoes would have been tempted to believe that lie. Nothing was adding up. On the one hand, the visit could not have been a farce because Samuel knew God sent him there. But if God was in on this, why was the anointing process so chaotic? Even a prophet with Samuel's sterling reputation would have to wonder after the third or fourth or seventh rejection whether the whole thing was a bust.

God, however, had not set up His prophet to fail. He simply brought Samuel to the end of himself, where no earthly idea could overshadow the divine plan. From that perch, Samuel heard God's hint: "Ask Jesse if he has another son."

The idea of an eighth son had not occurred to Samuel. Like the imminent leap in governance, the emergence of an eighth son decimated all kinds of paradigms: It opened Samuel to an unimagined outcome. It forced Jesse to come clean and recalibrate his view of David as an "insignificant" son. It obliterated David's position as the family outcast and turned the table on his brothers, who would now have to accept David's exalted status. It catapulted Samuel over the grief of Saul's failure. It also vanquished Jesse's resistance and released the great leap forward that God desired for Israel.

When they are obeyed, divine directives release transformation. They jettison our unconscious tendencies to protect the status quo, or nurse our fears of the unknown, or judge present and future experiences on the basis of the known past. Just as God's *no* moved Samuel toward the decision that released God's desired outcome, His divine directives—*when obeyed*—lead us to whatever is next in His plan.

THE DEAD PROPHETS SOCIETY

The process does not always run like clockwork. We don't know exactly how close Samuel came to throwing up his hands and walking away. And before we castigate Jesse, we need to remember how many times we have missed the magnitude of what God was doing in our lives. We read the Bible with the benefit of hindsight, but Jesse lived it the way we live—imperfectly and unevenly. Who knows what distractions had him bound or to what degree his own wounds caused him to live on autopilot?

The price was the same for Samuel and Jesse as it is for us. When we repeat the known past, whether through intentional disobedience or a lack of understanding (or both), we suffer a loss that is deducted from our future outcomes. So we need to search our hearts and ask: Are we rejecting the unexpected alternatives God offers us? Or are we choosing to become modern sons and daughters of Issachar—a company of strong donkeys and burden-bearers who can understand the times and participate with Him in the future outcomes He has in mind?

The latter is God's dream for us and for His world. He has never sought a company of cultural giants who stand head and shoulders above everyone else. He seeks imperfect but open-hearted men and women who are willing to work hard, plow their assigned fields, and cultivate their understanding of the times on His terms instead of their own. If we will ask Him, He will train us to function at a level of understanding that empowers us to train and lead others. He will give us the insight we need to recognize the future He has in mind and to know what to do in every situation.

THERE IS A REWARD

In the midst of the shaking that seems to portend doom, the promises of God are alive, well, and packed with limitless potential to create previously unimagined futures. To perceive God's alternatives to the known past is to first hear His voice and *expect a future*. As with all aspects of God's kingdom, faith is the access key. God's promises are for us, but they don't automatically drop their fulfillment into our laps. Nor are they fulfilled because they are good. To experience God's alternative future, we have to *act as if* His promises are absolutely, 100 percent trustworthy, even when the answers seems to be, "No. No. No. No. No. No. No."

A people with this mind-set is by definition one that quits recycling past experiences. The creation of unknown futures demands that we crush the habit-driven ways that keep us from God's promises, bind us to the familiar, and prevent us from anticipating anything new. If we, the Church, will pay heed, there will be portents of a coming reformation—a revolution, so to speak, spearheaded by men and women who have been set aside and told they are "insignificant." Though they are largely unnoticed and often undervalued, they faithfully plow their fields and bow their shoulders to carry the burdens that others ignore—the ones God has been waiting for His people to take up.

God rewards such diligence.[15] It is interesting that the name *Issachar* means "there will be recompense" and "he will bring a reward."[16] Revelation 19:10 says that "the testimony of Jesus is the spirit of prophecy." The strong donkey (which literally and figuratively carries The Prophet and Bread from heaven through Jerusalem's gates) receives the prophet's reward. The same sons of Issachar who work the land and protect the sheep are those who lead God's people up the sacred mountain to receive revelation and share in His bounty.

Of Zebulun he said, "Rejoice, Zebulun, in your going forth, and, Issachar, in your tents. They will call peoples to the mountain; there they will offer righteous sacrifices; for they

---

15. Heb. 11:6.

16. *Strong's Hebrew Lexicon*, Blue Letter Bible, s.v. "Yissaskar," (Strong's H3485), accessed February 8, 2017, https://www.blueletterbible.org//lang/lexicon/lexicon.cfm?Strongs=H3485&t=KJV.

will draw out the abundance of the seas, and the hidden treasures of the sand."[17]

What is required for the saints to rebuild the altar of God and offer their lives as fresh sacrifices? There has to be an understanding of the times and seasons, a recognition of patterns, and an anticipation of what wants to unfold. Some may choose to water down the gospel in an effort to please all comers; but participating in a vanguard would involve unashamedly choosing to please the Master. This entails refusing to manipulate or adulterate the Scriptures, even if those who choose otherwise find occasion to deride such refusal.

The Church, as God's prophetic vanguard company is to be dedicated to restoring others rather than protecting themselves. To have an Issachar mind-set requires being staunch proponents of life in what Pope John Paul II referred to as a "culture of death"[18] Such a company is unconcerned with asking, "What's in it for us?" Their question becomes, "What's in it for our Father?"

------

17. Deut. 33:18–19.

18. "The actual term 'Culture of Death' first entered common use after Pope John Paul II mentioned it several times in the 1993 encyclical, Evangelium Vitae...one of the timeliest and influential writings John Paul II produced during his pontificate. Evangelium Vitae is Latin for 'the Gospel of Life.' In this encyclical, John Paul II wrote about the intrinsic value of every human life, which must be welcomed and loved from the moment of conception to the moment of natural death. Here is a quote from this great encyclical: 'This situation, with its lights and shadows, ought to make us all fully aware that we are facing an enormous and dramatic clash between good and evil, death and life, the "culture of death" and the "culture of life." We find ourselves not only "faced with" but necessarily "in the midst of" this conflict: we are all involved and we all share in it, with the inescapable responsibility of choosing to be unconditionally pro-life.'" John I, "What Is the Culture of Death? (The Catholic Meaning)," A Solemn Charge, October 19, 2012, accessed February 8, 2018, http://www.solemncharge.com/post/2012/10/19/What-is-the-Culture-of-Death-The-Catholic-Meaning.aspx.

Seeking no recognition as kings, a vanguard is content to carry their King into the next generation. These strong donkeys are pleased to lie down between the sheepfolds for the sake of the flock. And because they understand the times and the age, they themselves are coming of age, for such a time as this.

CHAPTER 3

TIME AND TIMES

IT HAS BEEN SAID that "timing is everything." While the statement is debatable, the importance of time and timing is indisputable. Imagine how our churches benefit when leaders recognize endings, transitions, and beginnings. How would stewarding such insights help pastors to shepherd their flocks more effectively, dismiss unnecessary distractions, and demystify uncertainties?

According to First Chronicles 12:32, the sons of Issachar "understood the times, with knowledge of what Israel should do." In the original Hebrew, the word translated "times" is a figure of speech that can refer to a single event or a continual occurrence.[1] In Scripture the word is used in a variety of ways to denote a "usual...proper...suitable...[or] appointed time,"[2] as well as "experiences, fortunes...occurrence...[and] occasions."[3] The word can refer to a specific event as well as the events and seasons leading up to it.

Many events formed the long delay between God's original promise of David's reign and the actual end of Saul's. It might have seemed that God had forgotten His promise, but God is

---

1. The English transliteration is *eth* (pronounced *ayth*).

2. "6256. eth," Bible Hub, accessed February 8, 2017, http://biblehub.com/hebrew/6256.htm.

3. Ibid.

not forgetful. The fact is that transitions are messy, and we are prone to shunning them. The belief that change equals loss is deeply embedded in the human psyche. Therefore, even beneficial change often meets with strong resistance.

Regardless of our resistance, change comes. Saul's death made change inevitable for Israel and for Saul's own household. Transition was unavoidable. Yet even with Saul's passing, the houses of Saul and David remained at war.[4] It took time to "make David king,"[5] but God's promise would not be denied.

MASTERING THE LIMINAL STATE

Liminal is a word with multiple applications. For our purposes, it means "of, relating to, or being an intermediate state, phase, or condition."[6] The keen prophetic awareness of the sons of Issachar equipped them to master the liminal state between God's promise and its fulfillment. They accepted the uncertainty and ambiguity inherent in a transfer of power and brought to the transition the assurance and clarity that were grounded in God's intent. They *knew* what wanted to happen and they cooperated with it. Therefore, "God's promise, that seemed to have been forgotten, eventually came to fruition."[7] Understanding the times helps us to master our liminal states.

---

4. 2 Sam. 3:1

5. 1 Chron. 12:38

6. Merriam-Webster Online, *Merriam-Webster Online Dictionary 2017,* s.v. "liminal," accessed May 23, 2017, https://www.merriam-webster.com/dictionary/liminal.

7. Cyril J. Barber, *1 Chronicles: The Faithfulness of God to His Word Illustrated in the Lives of the People of Judah,* Focus on the Bible Commentary (Scotland: Christian Focus Publications, 2004), 145.

TIME OR TIMES?

We commonly speak of "the times in which we live" and compare them to the way things were "in days past." When we compare our *times* with another *time*, we are dealing with more than singular and plural versions of the word.

TIME

Time exists within God Himself. Consider the late Robert W. Jenson's accounting of Karl Barth's view of time as it relates to God and man:

> According to Barth, God in himself is not atemporal, but temporal. The time which He, in his eternal life, has is the possibility and model of created time. There exists however this fundamental difference between God's time and created time as such: In God past, present and future are not separated; in merely creaturely time they fall apart into a succession of separate "times."[8]

Jenson adds that "God is indeed eternally present to all creatures. But although they and their time are enclosed in God's eternal time, they are in their time and not in his. Jesus Christ is in God's time."[9]

Scholarly views of time and eternity are debatable, but God's command of them is not. The eternal God declares His intent, even declaring the end from the beginning.[10] On the fourth day of the Creation, He said, "Let there be lights in the expanse of the heavens to separate the day from the night, and let them be for signs and for seasons and for days and years."[11] On that "day," God established the framework within which

---

8. Robert W. Jenson, "Cur Deus Homo? The Election of Jesus Christ in the Theology of Karl Barth" (doctoral diss., University of Heidelberg, 1959), 53.

9. Ibid., 87.

10. Isa. 46:10.

11. Gen. 1:14.

humankind could measure the increments of time—the years, months, weeks, days, minutes, and seconds as we know them. Heavenly bodies were (and still are) the signs humanity used to track time's passage and to plan for the future. It took centuries to note and codify the recurring patterns that signal the times of day and rotation of seasons. But the understanding proved invaluable, especially where agriculture and the tides are concerned.

Broadly speaking, we divide time into past, present, and future. We live in time but cannot control its passage. We travel in time as the earth does, but apart from remembering the past, we can only move forward in time. Through the millennia, humanity has standardized and improved its time measurement technologies, yet each of us "measures" time differently. To the child who would rather play in the sunshine, an hour of assigned reading feels like an eternity. To the lifelong learner with scarce discretionary time, an hour of reading evaporates far too quickly.

TIMES

The span from the beginning of time to its consummation is comprised of times that are both sequential and overlapping, so that the times in which we live are connected to the times in which our predecessors lived *and* the times in which our descendants will live. This is the biblical sense of *the times*: the term speaks to the present as well as to what preceded and follows it.

As Torah scholars, the sons of Issachar understood this idea. They reached into the known past in order to interpret the present and create a previously unknown future. They measured current conditions against God's prophetic promises and the potential those promises offered. Their approach within time cooperated with God's eternal perspective. They had the hindsight to understand where God had been, the insight to know where He was in the present, and the foresight to perceive where He was headed.

The times are about more than time itself. Wrapped into the times are the conditions we experience and the dynamic outcomes that our decisions make possible. Despite popular ideas about God's sovereignty, being in God's will does not mean responding robotically to Him. Many futures are possible in the unfolding of the divine will. As the American theologian and semiotician Dr. Leonard Sweet, says, "No one discovers the future. The future is not a discovery. The future is not a destiny. The future is a decision, an intervention....The future is a function of our choices and creations."[12]

Dr. Sweet's point is well taken. The future is not a fixed outcome awaiting discovery. God has not asked us to *find* His will, but to *prove* it:

> *Therefore I urge you, brethren, by the mercies of God, to present your bodies a living and holy sacrifice, acceptable to God, which is your spiritual service of worship. And do not be conformed to this world, but be transformed by the renewing of your mind, so that you may* **prove what the will of God is, that which is good and acceptable and perfect**.[13]

With every choice, we progressively prove the future, using the innate anticipation that causes us to assess the current seasons and conditions and decide accordingly. This is at least in part what Len Sweet means when he says the future is an intervention. The intervention occurs in the *now* and creates a future that our "detector" says is possible.

These interventions happen every day, often in mundane ways. Your morning commute is a good example. Based on present conditions, previous experiences, and the weather

---

12. Leonard Sweet, *SoulTsunami: Sink or Swim in New Millennium Culture* (Grand Rapids: Zondervan, 1999), 55.

13. Rom. 12:1–2.

(among other things), you anticipate how long your commute will take on a given day, and you decide on a suitable departure time. God does not typically dictate these choices; He has given you the capability and latitude to decide for yourself. Therefore, depending upon when you leave the house, which route you choose, how accurate weather reports are, how slow or fast you drive, and whether or not you stop for coffee on the way, many outcomes are possible.

This is the essence of an open rather than closed system. Humanity is an open system and will remain so until all things are summed up in Christ. When the restoration purchased at Calvary is complete, God's plan will have been fulfilled. Amazingly, all of the choices made by human beings throughout the ages will be divinely woven into the tapestry of His eternal purpose, which was established before time began.

POSSIBLE, PROBABLE, PREFERRED, AND PLAUSIBLE FUTURES[14]

The ancient sons of Issachar anticipated the future, much the way present-day futurists and others engage in scenario planning to answer these key questions:

- What might happen in the future?
- Realistically speaking, what future do I desire?

In anticipating future scenarios, four categories are typically considered: (1) the possible, (2) the probable, (3) the preferable, and (4) the plausible. The *possible future* is the broadest, least constricted category, which includes anything that might happen. *Probable futures* are discovered analytically, by studying causal factors and

---

14. This brief discussion of exploring future possibilities is based on the following work: Greg Githens, "How to Use the 4Ps to Capture Future Scenarios: Thinking Strategically," March 26, 2013, The Strategic Thinking Coach, accessed May 26, 2017, https://strategicthinkingcoach.com. An application of these ideas will be offered in Chapter 4.

events. *Preferred future* states are those you want to see happen. (This assumes that you can influence the future and make choices that would support your preference.) The optional category of *plausible futures* narrows the range of future states in the *possible* category by isolating outcomes that appear to be valid based on what is already known.

THE TIMES AND OUR HORIZON

Have you ever heard people say that "the sun rises and sets" on their loved ones? The metaphor expresses the centrality of certain people in their lives. The obvious reference is to the sun, which literally (albeit visually) rises and sets on the horizon. This pattern makes the horizon a reference point by which human beings have distinguished between east and west, the times of day, and even the seasons.

The late T. Austin-Sparks describes an even more consequential horizon in the following verses:

*He commanded us to preach to the people, and to testify that it is He who was **ordained** by God to be Judge of the living and the dead.*[15]

*He has appointed a day on which He will judge the world in righteousness by the Man whom He has **ordained**. He has given assurance of this to all by raising Him from the dead.*[16]

In both cases the English word *ordained* is the transliterated word *horizō* in the Greek. Its literal meaning is "determine horizons,"[17] and it "refers to the Lord (literally) 'horizoning'

---

15. Acts 10:42 (NKJV).

16. Acts 17:31 (NKJV).

17. "3724.horizó," Biblehub.com, accessed January 25, 2018, http://biblehub.com/greek/3724.htm.

all the physical scenes of life before creation. This guarantees God works each in conjunction with His eternal purpose."[18]

According to Austin-Sparks, these verses from the Book of Acts state "that God has designated His Son—Jesus Christ—as the ultimate Horizon and Criterion of all judgment. That means that Christ is to be the sphere and scope, the realm and the range within whom and according to whom all things will be determined."[19]

You could say that the sun rises and sets on Christ, the Horizon by which the living and the dead will be judged. He is our reference point, the "Criterion of all judgment,"[20] the One by whom we judge all things, including our understanding of the times. Austin-Sparks notes the implications:

> This introduces a quite serious element into life, especially the life of the Christian. Sooner or later, every true Christian, i.e. every born-anew child of God, will find that the Spirit of God is pressing this criterion against his or her life.[21]

Horizons are also studied in the secular realms of "futures work and long-term thinking,"[22] where *horizon scanning* is used to assess what lies ahead. Horizon scanners look forward by "systematically exploring the external environment to: better understand the nature and pace of change in that environment; and, identify potential opportunities, challenges and likely future developments relevant to [an] organisation."[23]

---

18. Ibid.

19. T. Austin-Sparks, *Horizoned by Christ,* Chapter 1, posted on the Online Library of T. Austin-Sparks, accessed May 16, 2017, http://www.austin-sparks.net/english/books/001881.html.

20. Ibid.

21. Ibid.

22. "Future Thinking," Centre for Future Studies, accessed May 17, 2017, http://www.futurestudies.co.uk/our-futures-thinking-portfolio/horizon-scanning/.

23. Ibid.

The ancient sons of Issachar would likely have taken such matters into account as they guided the "organization" known as Israel through the transition between the reigns of Saul and David. They accurately assessed the external environment and the changes that were underway. They recognized the opportunity (to officially make David king), and they understood the challenges they faced. They also recognized that the changes being made externally had to be processed internally. That is essentially what transition is—the internal process of an external change.

The processing of the transition was uneven. Those who resisted the rise of David were not particularly interested in scanning the horizon. Their focus was fixed on the past they wanted to preserve (the "change as loss" mind-set). Meanwhile, the sons of Issachar recognized the external changes as opportunities for growth and positioned themselves and Israel to successfully navigate the transfer of power.

The inherent tension between those who favored the status quo and those who anticipated a previously unknown future delayed David's ascension to Israel's throne.[24] At some point change prevailed and the transition was complete.

SCANNING TO ANTICIPATE

In the marketplace, horizon scanning is the building of "knowledge of the relevant trends in the external environment that are likely to have a significant impact on the way it does business in the future, and the implications of those trends on the organisation's strategy to-

---

24. In the transition between Saul's death and the fulfillment of God's promise of David as king, Saul's son Ish-bosheth was made king over Israel, while Judah remained faithful to David. Ish-bosheth's own tragic end made way for God's promise to reach its ultimate fulfillment. 1 Sam. 31; 2 Sam. 2:10; 2 Sam. 4.

day."[25] Horizon scanning helps organizations to anticipate changing environments and "create their preferred
future."[26]

How might horizon scanning reveal changing landscapes
and empower God's vanguard to anticipate and move toward a preferable future?

TIME, TIMES, AND LEAPS

In Chapter 1, we saw a link between unexpected seasons of
tumult and great leaps forward. When the shaking is divine,
the breaking down of *what is* produces a springing forward
into *what's next*. These leaps can be monumental and para-
digm-destroying, but because we seem wired to resist change,
we often miss them.

Leaps *happen*, whether we perceive them or not. The term
quantum leap, which originated in the world of physics, is used
metaphorically in the culture to describe "an abrupt change,
sudden increase, or dramatic advance."[27] The invention of the
lightbulb and the advent of flight are good examples of great
leaps forward that altered perceptions of what was possible.
Other leaps are spurred by less welcome events, such as the at-
tacks of September 11, 2001. In that case, unthinkable carnage
led to shocking cultural, political, and geopolitical shifts that
previously seemed unimaginable.

In his book, *Into the New Age*, Anglican cleric and scholar Stephen Verney speaks of "evolutionary leaps," a concept
based on the work of American physicist and philosopher,
John R. Platt. Platt believed that quantum jumps are always

25. "Future Thinking," accessed May 25, 2017, http://www.futurestudies.
co.uk/our-futures-thinking-portfolio/horizon-scanning/.

26. Ibid.

27. Merriam-Webster Online, *Merriam-Webster Online Dictionary 2017*,
s.v. "quantum leap," accessed May 25, 2017, https://www.merriam-web-
ster.com/dictionary/quantum leap.

preceded by a sense of cognitive dissonance that builds and eventually demands resolution.

> First, there are accumulating bits of data that do not fit the old predictions, or rules of thumb in certain areas that seem to be justified only by odd assumptions. In the beginning, these difficulties are dismissed as trivial, or as errors of measurement or crack-pot arguments, but they do not go away, and they get more numerous.[28]

In the early twenty-first century, cognitive dissonance is in abundant supply. Traditional institutions are being tested. Confusion is rampant. Norms that have held for millennia are being recast and even rejected in some quarters. Roles and relationships are in flux, and emerging generations face challenges to their identity. These factors contribute to an increasingly complex way of life, which begs simplification and resolution.

The pressure caused by cognitive dissonance is seen throughout history. Platt explains how it precipitated the Protestant Reformation: "The first stages of the Reformation were attempts to reform the church from within because of the feeling of dissonance between its ideals and its practice."[29] The most well-known point of contention was the selling of indulgences, a transaction that granted forgiveness from sin in exchange for cash. The practice contradicted biblical ideals and contributed to a growing distrust of the papacy and the Church. The Reformers confronted the issue, not as a means of breaking with the Roman Church, but in the hopes of harmonizing its ideals and practices and restoring its legitimacy.

The Reformation did much more than reform the Church: it transformed Christendom. In Platt's and Verney's terms,

---

28. John Platt, "Hierarchical Restructuring," *Bulletin of Atomatic Scientists* (November 1970): 29, PDF reprint accessed May 25, 2017, http://www.radicalsoftware.org/volume2nr1/pdf/VOLUME2NR1_art06.pdf.

29. Ibid.

it was a quantum jump or evolutionary leap. While the term *evolutionary leap* is useful in identifying such movements, the term *revolutionary leap* would seem more precise, denoting separation from the theory of evolution. Either way, such leaps can happen at any time, creating what did not previously exist and simplifying whatever came before.[30]

Revolutionary leaps profoundly affect time by seeming to collapse it, so that advancements and transformations become virtually instantaneous.[31] Platt cites the example of the French Revolution, which transformed French thinking and overthrew traditional social and governmental structures in a matter of months.

A rational man would have said that any deep change would take fifty years or more, the time to train teachers, say, to re-educate the sons of the nobility, or the time to achieve ecclesiastical reform or a more sympathetic court. Yet, when the change came, it came like lightning, though final working-out took many years.[32]

Sudden, revolutionary leaps are unpredictable, but the continuity and consistency of God are steadfast. Even when a wild card upends expectations (as happened when Christopher Columbus's discovery of alternate trade routes decimated China's primacy or when World War I shifted power away from London to New York City), a vanguard company that understands the times can trust His unchangeableness and discern the leaps to be taken.

The greater the centrality of Christ in the believer's life, the more organic his or her leap-taking becomes. This can be likened to the way a tree trunk spontaneously shifts energy into

---

30. Platt, "Hierarchical Restructuring," 29.

31. As it is used here, *instantaneous* is a relative term. Hypothetically, if a star with a presumed life span of eight or ten billion years burns out after half a million years, its death might be considered instantaneous.

32. Platt, "Hierarchical Restructuring," 30.

branch production, or a leaf makes way for fruit with a sense of perfect timing. How do these structures know when to do these things, except that something in the divinely created order releases an impulse to leap? The shift is organic and seamless, producing something new out of something that already is.

POWER OF THE QUANTUM LEAP

In physics, a quantum leap involves the sudden movement of atomic particles from one energy level to another. The movement does not result from a previous state or condition; it just happens, and it can happen at any time. Although the distance traveled within an atom is infinitesimal, it is powerful. "Quantum leaps are the sole cause of the emission of electromagnetic radiation, including light, which occurs in the form of quantized units called *photons*."[33] Quantum leaps in culture, governance, the arts, and technology are similarly powerful. In fact, they are revolutionary.

FAITH NOW, FOR THE FUTURE

"When it comes to the future, the only thing one can be sure of is that common sense will be wrong."[34] Those are the words of George Friedman, the founder of Stratfor, a firm specializing in intelligence and forecasting in the realm of geopolitics and security. In Friedman's line of work, possibilities *must* be anticipated by thinking outside the proverbial box and into an unknown future.

---

33. "What Is a Quantum Leap?" Answers, accessed May 17, 2017, http://www.answers.com/Q/What_is_a_quantum_leap?#slide=2.

34. George Friedman, *The Next 100 Years: A Forecast for the 21ˢᵗ Century* (New York: Doubleday, 2009), 3.

For God's vanguard company, to think strategically about the future is a function of faith, understanding that God is a God of alternatives that run against the grain of the prevailing culture. The ancient sons of Issachar understood this and embraced what most of Israel either never perceived or chose to reject. Like Israel, we can mistakenly expect His visitation in our "high places" and be surprised when He visits Muslims in the far reaches of the globe. We can gather in stadiums and conferences and miss His movements among a diaspora of Syrians who have been brutalized by wicked forces and forgotten by much of the world.

Today's sons and daughters of Issachar can do what their ancient counterparts did for Israel. In understanding the times, the prophetic vanguard will more accurately discern where God is and where He is going. This comes only by *revelation*. It is received by faith, which operates in the *now* to reveal the truth of the present and future. This is how God meets His people and prepares them to master the times. He reveals Himself on His terms, within the context of His continuity and consistency, and often in the midst of the shakings that are meant to bring not destruction, but change.

It is important to stress that social, cultural, and economic tremors are not mere side effects of tumultuous times. They are signs that help us to see where God is going so we can cooperate and participate with Him. When we respond to shakings from this perspective, we will glorify Him from the midst of the chaos and accurately perceive the potential that is packaged within it.

God has told us to expect revolutionary leaps. He said, "Behold, I am doing a new thing; now it springs forth, do you not perceive it? I will make a way in the wilderness and rivers in the desert."[35] Yet when we enter wilderness and desert seasons, we often become convinced that all hope is lost. He

---

35. Isa. 43:19 (ESV).

understands and reminds us, "You desire and do not have, so you murder. You covet and cannot obtain, so you fight and quarrel. You do not have, because you do not ask."[36] He also promises that He "is able to do far more abundantly beyond all that we ask or think, according to the power that works within us."[37]

Taking God at His Word forms resolve in us. When the ground was bone-dry and the sky was cloudless, Elijah stepped out by faith and told King Ahab that he heard the "sound of abundance of rain."[38] The prophet bowed on the ground with his face between his knees, prayed, and told his servant to check the skies for rain. Six times, his servant found nothing. But the seventh time, he saw a "little cloud like a man's hand... rising from the sea."[39]

Elijah accurately perceived where God was going and therefore understood the times and glorified God before Ahab. We are invited to do the same. "There is an appointed time for everything. And there is a time for every event under heaven."[40] Scripture shows that God intends His people to discern the times. It is for us to ask Him, and He will answer us.

The past will not be changed. It *cannot* be changed. But when we understand the times that are past and accurately perceive the present time and the times in which we live, we will know how to seize the future for the sake of Jesus.

The kingdom of the world is becoming the kingdom of our Lord and of His Christ![41]

---

36. James 4:2 (ESV).

37. Eph. 3:20.

38. 1 Kings 18:41 (NKJV).

39. 1 Kings 18:44 (ESV).

40. Eccles. 3:1.

41. Rev. 11:15.

ASK TO SEE

If we are sons and daughters of Issachar, we can cultivate a clearer understanding of where we are and what the Church is facing in the short term (the next five to ten years). Asking the following questions will help us.

- What revolutionary leap is ahead and what shape is it taking?

- What is our sense of what needs to be done?

- Are people meeting Jesus in different ways?

- What changes will we need to make in the next five years, and what will be the effect on the local church?

CHAPTER 4

TRANSFER AND THE DOUBLE PORTION

THE PROPHETIC TRANSFER THAT BINDS the lives and ministries of Elijah and Elisha also powerfully illustrates how times and seasons that are centuries apart are vitally interconnected. American theologian Peter Leithart explains this brilliantly through typologies in the Elijah-Elisha narrative. Leithart proposes Elijah and Elisha as the "new Moses" and "new Joshua," but also as types of John the Baptist and Jesus, and Jesus and His disciples.[1] All of these relationships involve succession in the governance of God's people, and all of them involve miracles.

Elijah and Elisha saw Yahweh as the sole source of power, both for their *seeing* and *doing*. What they received by entering His sacred realms, they in turn conveyed to God's people, in the form of alternative futures. Although many prophetic voices spoke during Israel's history, Leithart suggests that the ministries of Elijah and Elisha "mark an epochal shift in the focus

---

1. Peter J. Leithart, *1 and 2 Kings*, Brazos Theological Commentary on the Bible, edited by R.R. Reno, Robert W. Jenson, Robert Louis Wilken, Ephraim Radner, Michael Root, and George Sumner (Grand Rapids: Baker, 2006), "2 Kings 2:1–25," Kindle Cloud Reader.

of Yahweh's work with Israel his people."[2] The shift involves God's choice of vessels: instead of working through the high priest or the king, He works through prophets.[3] "Ultimately, Yahweh's work through prophets comes to its fruition in the ministry of Jesus, who gathers a community within Israel, re-defining the true Israel as those who follow him as disciples."[4]

THE NEW MOSES

Elijah served in a season of broken covenant, when wicked leaders worshipped idols and the nation followed. Moses understood such breaches: he descended from his meeting with God on Mount Sinai to find the Israelites worshipping a golden calf. Enraged by their idolatry, Moses "threw the tablets [of the testimony] from his hands and shattered them at the foot of the mountain."[5] Nevertheless, Moses interceded for the people and asked God to forgive them.

Elijah also experienced grief over Israel's whoredom. Based on his revelation of the divine intent, he declared to Ahab a season of drought: "As the LORD, the God of Israel, lives, before whom I stand, there shall be neither dew nor rain these years, except by my word."[6] God did exactly as Elijah prophesied: He turned off the water. According to James 5:17, "it did not rain on the earth for three years and six months."

When God signaled the drought's end,[7] Elijah arranged a showdown between Baal and Yahweh. Like Moses, He stood firm against idolatry but interceded on behalf of the people,

---

2. Ibid., "1 Kings 17:1–24."

3. Ibid.

4. Ibid. Peter Leithart here relies also on the work of the great N. T. Wright, *Jesus and the Victory of God: Christian Origins and the Question of God* (London: SPCK, 1996).

5. Exod. 32:19.

6. 1 Kings 17:1 (ESV).

7. 1 Kings 18:1.

praying, "Answer me, O Lord, answer me, that this people may know that You, O Lord, are God, and that You have turned their heart back again."[8] His prayer reflected the divine will and brought heaven to earth on Mount Carmel.

Then the fire of the Lord fell and consumed the burnt offering and the wood and the stones and the dust, and licked up the water that was in the trench. When all the people saw it, they fell on their faces; and they said, "The Lord, He is God; the Lord, He is God."[9]

Elijah's words and acts entreated the people to return to God. They accepted his invitation by claiming Yahweh as their God.[10] The 850 prophets of Baal and Ashtoreth that had gathered at Elijah's request did not fare as well. Elijah killed every one of them. He then told Ahab that rain was coming, sent him away to eat a meal, and crouched in fierce intercession for the manifestation of what God had revealed.

Soon, the rain came. The victory was massive: The people had witnessed God's power and acknowledged Him as the true God. Jezebel's priests were slaughtered and the drought was over. Yet Elijah's sense of victory was short-lived. The seething Jezebel vowed to kill him within a day's time. Her retaliation signified more than her grievance against a man; it expressed her rejection of God and His covenant.

Jezebel's fury released torrents of demonic authority and activity. Devastated and utterly oppressed, Elijah ran for his life and sunk to suicidal levels of depression. In complete hopelessness, he slept under a broom tree in the wilderness. His work, however, was not yet finished:

The angel of the Lord came again a second time and touched him and said, "Arise and eat, for the journey is too great

---

8. 1 Kings 18:37.

9. 1 Kings 18:38–39.

10. Leithart, *1 and 2 Kings*, "1 Kings 18:1–46," Kindle Cloud Reader.

*for you." And he arose and ate and drank, and went in the strength of that food forty days and forty nights to **Horeb**, the mount of God. There he came to a cave and lodged in it. And behold, the word of the Lᴏʀᴅ came to him, and he said to him, "**What are you doing here, Elijah**?"*[11]

Horeb is Mount Sinai, where God's presence and glory once manifested in fire, smoke, and the shaking of the mountain.[12] God was bringing Elijah back to basics. At Horeb, He would show Elijah similar manifestations to those Moses and Israel had seen.[13] God also restored Elijah by recommissioning him with instructions to anoint Hazael as king of Syria, Jehu as king of Israel, and Elisha as prophet.

God's orders assured Elijah that Jezebel's days were numbered. He was now able to set aside his personal crisis and head to Abel-meholah, where Elisha lived.

THE NEW JOSHUA

If Elijah is the new Moses, Elisha is the "new Joshua."[14] Just as Moses designated Joshua as his successor, Elijah designated Elisha, the son of Shaphat, to succeed him.[15] He did it at Elisha's birthplace,[16] Abel-meholah (the "dance-meadow")[17] in the territory of Issachar.

This was an unlikely place for Elijah to find his successor. And, because he had no prior relationship with Elisha, this was not the "likely" candidate. Elisha had not traveled in ministry

11. 1 Kings 19:7–9 (ESV).

12. Exod. 19:18.

13. 1 Kings 19:11–12.

14. Leithart, *1 and 2 Kings*, "1 Kings 17:1–24," Kindle Cloud Reader

15. 1 Kings 19:16; Leithart, "1 Kings 17:1–24," Kindle Cloud Reader.

16. 1 Kings 19:16.

17. Francis Brown, Samuel Rolles Driver, and Charles Augustus Briggs, *Enhanced Brown-Driver-Briggs Hebrew and English Lexicon* (Oxford: Clarendon Press, 1977), 6.

circles. He was comfortable behind the plow, and he was dedicated to his business.

In the divine plan, however, the men were very much connected and shared a mutual impartation that released them both into the fullness of God's eternal purpose. Long before their first meeting, Elisha had almost certainly been primed for the connection.[18] It is unclear whether he expected Elijah to show up on *that* day. Clearly, however, he expected an encounter at some point—so much so that his future found him, and not the other way around!

The timing of the men's first meeting is telling. The prosperous Elisha was clearly not bound to outcomes that were predictable in times of drought and paucity. He generated wealth amid scarcity and had twelve yoke of oxen to prove it![19] Where others saw lack, Elisha saw possibility. He saw into unseen realms, and what he saw empowered him to sow, reap, and employ others.

This was exactly what Israel needed. Where the enemy had a stronghold, God provided a man who understood the times and what Israel must do. Elijah would mentor him just as Moses mentored Joshua. In the fullness of times, Elijah would depart knowing that his successor was in place.

ELISHA'S ISSACHAR HERITAGE

The time of the Elijah-Elisha narrative was pivotal in Israel's history. When the mantle finally changed hands, Issachar returned to the prophetic vanguard. Elijah, a precursor to John the Baptist, had largely focused on God's anger with His people, while Elisha, whom Peter Leithart compares to Jesus, presented alternatives to

---

18. God would not have sent Elijah on a questionable mission. Instead, He would have prepared the way by calling Elisha *before* He sent His prophet to designate him.

19. 1 Kings 19:19.

Israel's darkened situation. This is part of the Issachar legacy Elisha carried.

THE MEETING AND THE MANTLE

When Elijah found Elisha, he signified God's preordained and future transfer. He did it without saying a word.

So he [Elijah] *departed from there and found Elisha the son of Shaphat, who was plowing with twelve yoke of oxen in front of him, and he was with the twelfth.* **Elijah passed by him and cast his cloak upon him.**[20]

Elisha's unflinching submission seems to confirm that he knew why Elijah had come and why he threw his mantle on him. Before Elijah arrived, Elisha had apparently settled in his mind what his response to the prophet would be.

He left the oxen and ran after Elijah and said, "Let me kiss my father and my mother, and then I will follow you." And he said to him, "Go back again, for what have I done to you?" And he returned from following him and took the yoke of oxen and sacrificed them and boiled their flesh with the yokes of the oxen and gave it to the people, and they ate. Then he arose and went after Elijah and assisted him.[21]

The implications of the mantle were not mysterious to Elisha. In Israel, coats symbolized the possibilities and promises of God. For example, God prescribed very detailed garments (essentially a mantle) for His priesthood. Joseph's many-colored coat was the mantle under which Joseph dreamed of his destiny.[22] Adam and Eve originally wore the mantle of God's glory. When they disobeyed Him, He provided them with new "coats" of animal skins (a story unto itself).

---

20. 1 Kings 19:19 (ESV).

21. 1 Kings 19:20–21 (ESV).

22. Gen. 37:3–9.

Elijah's mantle was a simple garment of sheepskin or camel hair, but when it hit Elisha's shoulders, his entire future shifted. The prophetic act confirmed that his destiny was bigger than the running of his father's business, and it signaled, metaphorically, the casting of vision from one prophet to another. Even if Elisha anticipated the event, he could not have experienced it apart from his connection to Elijah. You could say the mantle was God's hook; it caught Elisha, commanded his awareness, and brought him into a fully-conscious understanding of his future.

Prophetic mantles are signs, but they also effect real change. Regardless of their wearers or the times in which they are worn, they have certain qualities in common:

1. *Mantles invoke awareness.*[23] When a mantle is received, it ignites a creative process and a fresh awareness of "something more." For Elisha, the invocation meant being able to touch that which, previously, he could only imagine.

2. *Mantles are activators; they provoke.* When the mantle hit Elisha's shoulders, it activated a new reality and provoked him to move toward his divinely-ordained future. Everything else *had* to shift.

3. *When mantles invoke, they also evoke* ("call forth or up").[24] Mantles call forth what is within; they also call it up and draw it out. Passions become stirred, and the mantle's wearer feels ruined for everything else. Elisha could not stay in his familiar life. He left his parents, sacrificed his oxen (his legacy to that point), and fed his sacrifice to his company. He also burned his plow, making it an altar for

---

23. "Invoke" is from the Latin, "*in-* + *vocare* to call." Merriam-Webster Online, *Merriam-Webster Online Dictionary 2017*, s.v. "invoke," accessed June 10, 2017, https://www.merriam-webster.com/dictionary/invoke.

24. Ibid., s.v. "evoke," accessed June 10, 2017, https://www.merriam-webster.com/dictionary/evoke.

his sacrifice. With every bridge burned behind him, he moved toward the double portion.

4. *Mantles awaken alternatives in a world of limited possibilities.* Under the prophetic mantle, a sanctified imagination sees past the prevailing struggles. Although the prophet acknowledges limiting factors, he or she will say, "Nevertheless, I have been given a promise, and it shall be fulfilled!"

THE NEW CREATION MANTLE

Today, the Holy Spirit and the Word of God are the believer's "mantle." We carry the Holy Spirit, not on our shoulders, but within us. When we speak God's Word, it is as though—to use the example of Elijah at the Jordan—we rolled up the mantle to form a rod and then used that rod to strike whatever "waters" we need to cross over. Outcomes are effected by the Holy Spirit when we speak and act by faith, trusting Him to do what He has already revealed and promised. When our confidence in God's Word wavers, we blunt its power and surrender His promises before they are fulfilled.

CONDITION FOR THE DOUBLE PORTION

We have seen evidence of how the Elijah-Elisha narrative reveals Elisha's awareness of God's purposes and timing. In Second Kings 2, Elijah perceived that his departure was imminent. He and Elisha were en route from Gilgal to Bethel; from there he planned to go to Jericho and the Jordan. Yet he urged Elisha not to accompany him to any of those places.

No doubt focused on the transfer of power and the double-portion of Elijah's prophetic spirit, Elisha refused to leave Elijah's side. Together, they arrived at the Jordan, where fifty sons of the prophets watched as "Elijah took his cloak and rolled it up and struck the water, and the water was parted to the one side and to the other, till the two of them could go over on dry ground."[25] (Bear in mind that Moses parted the Red Sea so Israel could cross over.)

After they crossed the river, Elijah's words seemed laden with heaviness:

"Ask what I shall do for you, before I am taken from you." And Elisha said, "Please let there be a double portion of your spirit on me." And he said, "You have asked a hard thing; yet, if you see me as I am being taken from you, it shall be so for you, but if you do not see me, it shall not be so."[26]

Elijah seemed unsure that he could deliver on Elisha's request, but well aware of what Elisha would have to do to receive it. They both knew a successor was needed, they knew who it was, and they knew that only Yahweh could confer the prophetic spirit. Elisha had learned to "earnestly desire the best gifts,"[27] but he did not stop there. He boldly asked for the double portion, which was already stirring in his heart. This was an act of faith, because the Mosaic Law denied the double portion to any but a firstborn son.[28]

Believing in the promise and its potential was one thing; seeing them fulfilled was another. To receive the double portion, Elisha would have to prove himself to be a visionary prophet. He would have to see Elijah being taken from him. It would be the kind of scene very few people had ever witnessed.

---

25. 2 Kings 2:8 (ESV).

26. 2 Kings 2:9–10 (ESV).

27. 1 Cor. 12:31 (NKJV).

28. Elisha surely knew that the requirement had been eased when Isaac gave the blessing to Jacob rather than Esau and when Jacob similarly blessed Ephraim instead of Manasseh.

THE TRANSFER

Elijah's final earthbound moments occurred at an invisible seam that was the gate of heaven itself. While the men walked and talked together, a supernatural drama unfolded. Despite its suddenness, neither man was caught unaware.

> *As they still went on and talked, behold, chariots of fire and horses of fire separated the two of them. And Elijah went up by a whirlwind into heaven. And Elisha saw it and he cried, "My father, my father! The chariots of Israel and its horsemen!" And he saw him no more. Then he took hold of his own clothes and tore them in two pieces.*[29]

Elisha proved himself to be the visionary prophet Elijah had hoped. Elisha saw the fiery horses and chariot and his mentor's exit from the earthly dimension. Both men had reached a point of no return. Elijah was no longer God's earthly representative. Elisha's former role had also ended, and his new life would require new garments. Symbolically discarding his former status, Elisha tore his clothes.

The transition was intense in every way, yet Elisha remained focused on the mantle. Notice the juxtaposition of ascents and descents: Elijah went up, and his mantle went up with him, passing into new dimensions which imbued it with new promise. Then, as Elisha watched, the mantle came down and Elijah disappeared into the heavenly realms.

Elisha retrieved the mantle, which was the only article of Elijah's that went up and came back down. The mantle was essential. It had to be preserved for the next generation and the new ordering of the kingdom. Because it briefly ascended into heavenly realms, Elisha would have a fresh awareness and appreciation of its value. He took the mantle, returned to the bank of the Jordan and, like his predecessor, struck the water

---

29. 2 Kings 2:11–12 (ESV).

with it, saying, "Where is the LORD, the God of Elijah?"[30] (Remember that Jordan had also parted for the passage of Joshua and the Israelites to enter the Promised Land.)[31]

Why, if Elisha was indeed a focused and visionary prophet who appreciated the mantle's value, did he ask where the "God of Elijah" was? The question is a human and transparent one. Elijah's ascent in the heavenly chariot (a throne, as we will see), makes the finality of his departure and the reality of Elisha's new season of unknowns all too clear.

Elisha's calling would require faith. Like any man or woman in a new role, and despite the fact that God deemed him qualified, Elisha felt no change within himself that assured him of his ability or worthiness to serve. Elisha asked about God's whereabouts because he wanted to know whether Elijah's God was with him *and* whether Yahweh was now the God of Elisha.

Elisha's ability to believe depended upon his spiritual perception, the condition upon which all spiritual work rests. We see his faith in his return to the scene of his mentor's last miracle—the striking of the water. It was now up to Elisha to smite the waters and cross over.

When he had struck the water, the water was parted to the one side and to the other, and Elisha went over. Now when the sons of the prophets who were at Jericho saw him opposite them, they said, "The spirit of Elijah rests on Elisha." And they came to meet him and bowed to the ground before him.[32]

Elisha's first prophetic act after Elijah's departure confirmed his calling. Whatever misgivings he experienced beforehand, it was now clear that his ministry was not based on his feelings of personal strength or self-confidence. He had stepped

---

30. 2 Kings 2:13–14b.

31. Josh. 3–4.

32. 2 Kings 2:14-15 (ESV).

forward in his weakness and now knew that he was called to operate in the power of God.

The sons of the prophets (who earlier wanted Elisha to know that they perceived his mentor's imminent departure) now recognized who Elisha was. Peter Leithart explains that the "sons of the prophets recognize the family resemblance between Elisha and his predecessor, just as the Jews perceive the courage of Peter and the apostles and remember they have been with Jesus (Acts 4:13)."[33]

Everyone could see that, although God had made changes to His leadership team, His power remained. The new prophet would pick up where his mentor had left off, to profound effect on the nation and on biblical history. Peter Leithart summarizes the Elijah-Elisha legacy:

> Elijah leaves a double portion of his spirit behind for Elisha, who begins to carry out a conquest of the land through healing and renewal, as well as judgment. When the work of these two prophets is done, there are organized communities of faithful worshipers within Israel.[34]

THE PROPHET'S FAITH

Elijah left Elisha in possession of the one thing he requested—the double portion. However, Elisha's active participation was mandatory.

- Elisha *saw* Elijah's exit.
- Elisha *seized* the fallen mantle.
- He *segued* back to smite the Jordan, cross it, and re-enter the Land.
- He *believed*; therefore, he spoke and acted.

---

33. Leithart, *1 and 2 Kings*, "2 Kings 2:1–25," Kindle Cloud Reader.

34. Leithart, *1 and 2 Kings*, "1 Kings 17:1–24," Kindle Cloud Reader.

STORM, WIND, AND FIRE THEOPHANIES AND CLOUD-CHARIOTS

Elijah said Elisha's request for the double portion was "a hard thing" that would only be possible if Elisha *saw*.[35] Elisha's response to his mentor's departure indicates that there was more to see than Elijah's exit. Elisha said, "My father, my father! The chariots of Israel and its horsemen!"[36] He witnessed a profound scene; "chariots of fire and horses of fire separated the two of them. And Elijah went up by a whirlwind into heaven."[37]

These dramatic elements of the story are not exclusive to the Elijah-Elisha narrative. They are seen throughout Scripture, because God appeared to His people many times and in ways they were not expecting. These appearances are called theophanies, and many of them share the features to which Elisha alludes.

For example, Isaiah wrote, "Behold, the Lord will come in fire and His chariots like the whirlwind."[38] Similarly, the psalmist explained that God "makes the clouds His chariot; He walks upon the wings of the wind."[39] Fire, wind, and chariots are not new to most Bible readers, but they are often overlooked or left unexplained.

Old Testament scholar John Day simply states that "Yahweh rides a cloud chariot."[40] The Hebrew word translated "chariots" in Second Kings 2:12 is *rekeb*, which speaks of a "chariot, i.e., a wheeled vehicle drawn by one or more horses, used for war or

---

35. 2 Kings 2:10 (ESV).

36. 2 Kings 2:12 (ESV).

37. 2 Kings 2:11 (ESV).

38. Isa. 66:15.

39. Ps. 104:3.

40. John Day, *Yahweh and the Gods and Goddesses of Canaan*, Journal for the Study of the Old Testament Supplement Series 265, edited by David J. A. Clines and Philip R. Davies (London: Sheffield Academic Press, 2000), Kindle Cloud Reader loc 1602.

travel."[41] The reason Elijah expressed uncertainty about Elisha's prophetic sight (remember that he said, "*If* you see...") was because the fiery chariot was not an earthly object. It was a vehicle of ascension that operated in the heavenly dimensions.

Previous chariots in Scripture were more "concrete" and typically involved in warfare. However, the chariot in Second Kings 2 was not engaged in war. This suggests it had a higher purpose, which for centuries has captivated the interest of Jewish mystics involved in *merkabah* study. *Merkabah*, which means "chariot," was mentioned in Second Chronicles 28:18, in a listing of items included in the temple plans that King David gave to Solomon. The verse mentions "his plan for the golden *chariot* of the cherubim that spread their wings and covered the ark of the covenant of the LORD."[42]

This verse links the *merkabah* to the Ark of God, and Jewish mystics have studied it in relation to God's throne. Some scholarship suggests that Saul's conversion on the Damascus Road was tied to merkabah practices.[43] The following excerpt from an academic paper encapsulates some of the biblical history of the throne-chariot:

> The basic elements of Jewish throne-chariot mysticism can be found in the biblical throne visions [see Exod. 24:10–11; 1 Kings 22:19; Isa. 6; Ezek. 1; 3:22–24; 8:1–18; 10:9–17; 43:1–4;

---

41. James Swanson, *Dictionary of Biblical Languages with Semantic Domains: Hebrew (Old Testament)* (Oak Harbor: Logos Research Systems, Inc., 1997).

42. 1 Chron. 28:18 (ESV).

43. Benjamin L. Fuller, "Throne-Chariot Mysticism and Paul: An Ancient Tradition's Influence on the Genius Who Brought Jesus to the World" (2012), 1–2. See also, J. W. Bowker, "'Merkabah' Visions and the Visions of Paul," *Journal of Semitic Studies* 16, no. 2 (October 1, 1971): 157–173, accessed January 18, 2018, https://academic.oup.com/jss/article-abstract/XVI/2/157/1715834/MERKABAH-VISIONS-AND-THE-VISIONS-OF-PAUL?redirectedFrom=fulltext.

Dan. 7:9–14]. Though there a[re] several examples, one of the most important comes from Ezekiel's theophany in which he receives his prophetic call vision by the river Chebar (Ezek. 1:2–28). Here the prophet Ezekiel gave an extensive yet cryptic depiction of what became known as the "throne-chariot," a kind of royal throne on wheels according to Daniel 7:9. Beginning with a stormy wind and a fiery cloud approaching from the north (v.4), Ezekiel's vision unfolds as a description of four bizarre "living creatures," each with four faces, four wings, and four wheels (vv.5–21). Above their heads was a platform like crystal (vv.22–25), and above the platform sat a manifestation of God on a sapphire throne described as "the appearance of the likeness of the glory of the Lord (vv.26–28)...."[44]

This is not a book about God's throne. The point here is that Elisha's success in receiving the double portion involved more than seeing Elijah leave. It demanded that he see into the heavenly realms and perceive the theophanies that other prophets witnessed.

ELISHA AND ALTERNATIVE FUTURES

In Chapter 3 we saw that God's sovereignty allows us to influence the future and intervene to create alternatives. We also explored four categories of futures: the possible, probable, preferable, and the plausible. Here we will focus on the first three, as they might relate to the Elijah-Elisha narrative.

Remember that Elijah gave his protégé multiple opportunities to stay behind as he (Elijah) traveled from Gilgal to Bethel, Jericho, and the Jordan.[45] Elisha was determined, however, to remain with his mentor. His persistence certainly affected

44. Fuller, "Throne-Chariot Mysticism and Paul," 1–2.

45. It is interesting to note that the places they visited was a reverse progression of Joshua's three key entry points as he led Israel into the land of promise. The Bethel mentioned in Second Kings 2 is not the Bethel where Jacob dreamed of the ladder from earth to heaven. It is a place located near

his outcome, although we cannot know exactly how *not* witnessing Elijah's departure would have impacted his future.

In the Elijah-Elisha narrative, then, the *possible* future was the broadest category, which allowed that an heir-apparent might exist. In that scenario, Elisha is only one possibility. One of the sons of the prophets might have been another. In hindsight, we know who God's choice was, but either man could have intervened by declining to cooperate. For example, what if Elijah perished in an extraneous battle not of God's choosing? Or what if Elisha had wandered from his land prematurely? It is conceivable that Elijah might have departed this life without designating a successor, leaving Elisha to run his business for the remainder of his lifetime.

The *probable* future was what the sons of the prophets and Elisha expected, which was Elijah's departure. They clearly expected to be separated from their leader, but that says little about who would succeed him. This is where Elisha's decisions came into play: he was not passive and certainly not interested in possible or probable futures. Elisha had a specific *preferable* future in mind that was based on what God had shown him (the promise). Elisha took the promise to heart and made choices that supported it.[46]

If we have preferable futures in mind, their fulfillment will require us to be equally steadfast, knowing that God's power was not exclusive to Elijah and Elijah or tied to a particular era. His power is eternal in both presence and availability. The God who parted the waters for Joshua as Israel entered the Promised Land, parted it for both Elijah and Elisha centuries

---

Ai, where Achan took forbidden articles and brought a curse upon himself and Israel.

46. In future studies, there is always the possibility of a wild card, an out-of-the-blue, game-changing event. A possible wild card would have been Elisha's rejection, despite all he knew and claimed to desire, of the double portion.

later. God's power was not paralyzed by Israel's idolatrous condition; nor is it prevented by today's corrupting influences.

God still saves, delivers, heals, sanctifies, speaks, and leads. He is not only the God of history, but the God of our times and our children's times. He cannot be restrained by evil or discouraged by sin. He is always powerful and always eager to work in and through a prophetic people who *see* and *act* in accordance with His will.

CHAPTER 5

THE CHARISMATIC SPIRIT AND THE PROPHETIC IMAGINATION

ECAUSE OF THE CHARISMATIC MOVEMENT of the twentieth century, many view the charismatic spirit as a twentieth- and twenty-first century "experience." In reality, the charismatic spirit, which is inseparable from the prophetic spirit, is also one with the spirit of prophecy, which is the testimony of Jesus,[1] the Holy Spirit Himself. Therefore, *charismatic* describes men like Elijah and Elisha, two "notable charismatic prophets,"[2] with whom Jesus, the ultimate charismatic Prophet, deeply identified.

Jesus explained how the ministries of His charismatic forerunners foreshadowed His own:

Truly I say to you, no prophet is welcome in his hometown. But I say to you in truth, there were many widows in Israel in

---

1. Rev. 19:10.

2. Stronstad, *Prophethood*, 40.

the days of Elijah, when the sky was shut up for three years and six months, when a great famine came over all the land; and yet Elijah was sent to none of them, but only to Zarephath, in the land of Sidon, to a woman who was a widow. And there were many lepers in Israel in the time of Elisha the prophet; and none of them was cleansed, but only Naaman the Syrian.[3]

Jesus understood that no prophet would be universally received and respected. Even people on the verge of starvation or plagued by leprosy had rejected the prophets God sent to help them. In this, Jesus compared Himself to His predecessors, and received exactly what He described—rejection. His words so offended the religious class that they plotted to throw Him off a cliff.[4]

By mentioning the widow of Zarephath and Naaman the Syrian, Jesus reminded Jews that although many had rejected God's servants in the past, there was always a remnant who embraced the prophetic and experienced the promise. He was offering His hearers a choice: they could become early adaptors or they could deny Him. Either way, He would do the Father's will and focus on those who would receive Him.

This choice is still ours to make. Although our charismatic Prophet did not drop a camel-hair garment as He ascended to heaven, He did promise to clothe us "with power from on high."[5] On the Day of Pentecost, He left us His Spirit and allowed us to share in the things He experienced in Luke chapters 3 and 4: the baptism in the Holy Spirit; the release into ministry; and the temptation.

Jesus's baptism in the Jordan was significant and is paralleled by Pentecost, in its significance to His Church. Theologian

---

3. Luke 4:24–27.

4. "He came to His own, and those who were His own did not receive Him." John 1:11.

5. Luke 24:29 (ESV).

Ray Anderson states that if "the Great Commission gives the Church its instructions; Pentecost provides its initiation and power."[6] To instruct the Church but not empower it would be unjust and unlike God. Instead, Pentecost ensured the viabiliate. Anderson elaborates:

> Pentecost is the pivotal point from which we can look back to the incarnation of God in Jesus of Nazareth and look forward into our contemporary life and witness to Jesus Christ in the world. Pentecost is more than a historical and instrumental link between a theology of the incarnation and a theology of the institutional church. Pentecost is more than the birth of the church; it is the indwelling power of the Spirit of Christ as the source of the church's life and ministry.[7]

NEW TESTAMENT SONS OF THE PROPHETS

Before his dramatic departure, Elijah prepared the spiritual ground by establishing schools of the prophets in known strongholds of idolatry. During his inaugural sermon on the Day of Pentecost, Peter related the early sons of the prophets to all of Jesus's disciples:

> *All the prophets who have spoken, from Samuel and his successors onward, also announced these days. It is you who are* **the sons of the prophets** *and of the covenant which God made with your fathers, saying to Abraham, "And in your seed all the families of the earth shall be blessed."*[8]

As sons of the prophets and image-bearers of Christ, our function is intrinsically prophetic and inseparable from our speaking. Clothed in Jesus's mantle, we are called to speak beyond ourselves. Jesus modeled this for us, saying, "I have

---

6. Ray S. Anderson, *The Soul of Ministry: Forming Leaders for God's People* (Louisville, KY: Westminster John Knox Press, 1997), 111.

7. Ibid.

8. Acts 3:24–25.

not spoken on my own authority, but the Father who sent me has himself given me a commandment—what to say and what to speak."[9] Jesus also said, "It is the Spirit who gives life; the flesh is no help at all. The words that I have spoken to you are spirit and life."[10]

Prophetic speech is more forth-telling than foretelling, speaking to the desires of the Father's heart and releasing or *loosing*[11] what is needed to accomplish them. In contrast to divination, it is a demonstration of our belief in God's promises, their potential, and our obedience. By the Spirit we believe and obey, and by the Spirit our obedience releases the potential inherent in the promise.

This idea was illustrated when Jesus instructed Simon Peter to find the temple tax in the mouth of a fish: "Go to the sea and cast a hook and take the first fish that comes up, and when you open its mouth you will find a shekel. Take that and give it to [the tax collectors] for me and for yourself."[12] Some call this a word of knowledge by which Jesus described a future event. That may very well be. However, as with all of Jesus's signs and wonders, this miracle demonstrates the reality of Jesus's words: "My Father is always working, and so am I."[13]

In other words, the divine renewing and other acts upon the Creation did not end in Genesis 2. The Son's statement reveals that He and the Father continue to exercise authority and creative power over the Creation, which is in the Almighty's hands. Jesus's utterance to Peter released processes that would result in the fulfillment of what He said. Understood in

---

9. John 12:49 (ESV).

10. John 6:63 (ESV).

11. The idea of binding and loosing (Matt. 16:19) is less about disabling demons and delivering captives than it is about binding us to the Father's will and loosing His power to fulfill it.

12. Matt. 17:27 (ESV).

13. John 5:17 (NLT).

the light of how the Father and Son labor together, this is not a foretelling as much as a forth-telling.

As New Testament sons of the prophets (and especially of *The* Prophet), we are to do what Jesus did, which is what His predecessors, Elijah and Elisha, did: they spoke beyond themselves, healing the sick, cleansing lepers, and raising the dead.[14] They functioned in the prophetic spirit, which means they moved in the Holy Spirit. When we do this, we cannot help but be expanded. He wants to expose us to divine realities that exceed our limitations and take us into the limitless realm of heaven, the "home of the possibles."[15]

GOD'S PROPHETIC CRAFTSMEN

When God commissioned His Tabernacle, He personally filled two men with His Spirit in "wisdom, in understanding, in knowledge, and in all kinds of craftsmanship...that they may make all that I have commanded you."[16] God expanded the men's thought processes, exposing them to His realities and moving them beyond their limitations. He shared everything they needed to know to fulfill the Tabernacle's promise. In Moses's Old Testament context, the men known as Bezalel and Oholiab were the "apostles and prophets" upon whom the foundations of the Tabernacle were built.[17]

---

14. 2 Kings 5:1–19. There are physical lepers and figurative ones. The latter are those who are being tormented in some way, eaten alive by some issue, situation, fear, or condition of the heart. 1 Kings 17:17–24.

15. Walter Wink, *Naming the Powers: The Language of Power in the New Testament* (Philadelphia: Fortress Press, 1984), 119.

16. Exod. 31:2–3, 6.

17. See Eph. 2:20.

INSEPARABLE: FATHER, SON, AND HOLY SPIRIT

There is something lacking in the way many Pentecostals and Charismatics discuss revival and reformation: it is the absence of clear language about the shared life of the Trinity. While many Evangelicals diminish and marginalize the scope of the Holy Spirit's work, many Pentecostals and Charismatics so strongly emphasize the Spirit, that the place of the Father and the Son is neglected.

Given that the Spirit *proceeds* from the Father through the Son, this neglect distorts the scriptural reality. When we speak of the Spirit apart from His relation to the Father and the Son, we seem to forget the Trinity. In the name of "mystery," we make excuses for our error and for our failure to teach (1) about the shared life and relationships within the Godhead, and (2) about the individual roles of the Father, Son, and Holy Spirit in the work of redemption.

On reflection, the pattern is predictable. Many have taught that the Trinity cannot be understood; therefore, many more assume that the Godhead is unknowable by design. Yet, if we consider the Incarnation, this argument falls apart. Jesus did not come to hide the Father or the Holy Spirit. He came to reveal the Father and leave us His Spirit! Therefore, choosing *not* to teach God's people about the Trinity is a disservice to them and to the Son's message. We must teach it, humbly confessing that our words are feeble at best and hard-pressed to describe the wonder of the Godhead.

The most obvious reality of the Trinity may be how profoundly relational the Father, Son, and Holy Spirit are—three Persons in one God, continuously interacting with one another, each distinct but not independent. We know Jesus never acted independently of the Father. Instead, He said, "The Son can do nothing of Himself, unless it is something

He sees the Father doing; for whatever the Father does, these things the Son also does in like manner."[18]

Bearing in mind that entire volumes cannot fully explain the Trinity, a simple way to understand it would be to say that the Father *thinks,* the Son *speaks,* and the Spirit *does.* There is no confusion or competition. Each member of the Godhead is satisfied in His role, always yielding to the others in love and honor. The paradox, to the human mind, is that despite their roles or yielding, there is no separation of the three Persons in any of their dealings. So, for example, Father, Son, and Holy Spirit were all involved in raising Jesus from the dead.[19] Although we find it difficult to balance these ideas, the members of the Godhead do not, as Paul explains through the example of the Son:

Have this attitude in yourselves which was also in Christ Jesus, who, although He existed in the form of God, did not regard equality with God a thing to be grasped, but emptied Himself, taking the form of a bond-servant, and being made in the likeness of men.[20]

Paul said the Son emptied Himself. However, the communion within the Godhead is a continual pouring of the Father into the Son and the Son into the Father through the agency of the Holy Spirit. (Note that He is called the Spirit of the Father and the Spirit of the Son, but not the Spirit of the Spirit.)

While there is a continual begetting between the Father and the Son,[21] the Spirit searches the Father and testifies of the Son. Through the Spirit, we enter into the ongoing communication between them. The Father loves the Son and the Son loves the Father; not within the limits of divine interaction but *through us.* This is what we sense during transcendent

---

18. John 5:19.

19. Rom. 6:4; Gal. 1:1; John 2:18–21; 10:18; Rom. 8:11; 1 Pet. 3:18.

20. Phil. 2:5–7.

21. John 1:18.

moments of worship when the weight of God's love presses us into Him. It is the apex of the Christian experience: the Father revealing the Son to us, the Son revealing the Father to us, and the Spirit revealing the Son *in* us.

The structure of God's household, the Church, highlights the interplay within the Godhead. Paul describes this in his letter to the Ephesians:

> ***Through Him*** [Christ] ***we both*** [Jew and Gentile] ***have our access in one Spirit to the Father.*** *So then you are no longer strangers and aliens, but you are fellow citizens with the saints, and are members of the household of God, built on the foundation of the apostles and prophets, Christ Jesus Himself being the cornerstone, in whom the whole structure, being joined together, grows into a holy temple in the Lord. In him you also are being built together into a dwelling place for God by the Spirit.*[22]

Verse 18, which is emphasized, summarizes the Trinitarian formula. The balance of the passage connects the Church to the temple, which was built according to God's ordained pattern and was the place where His glory came down.

PERICHORESIS

The Trinity has been described as a divine dance. The word *perichoresis*, literally means "rotation"[23] and describes how each member of the Godhead "penetrates the others and is penetrated by them."[24] According to Alistair McGrath, "[Perichoresis] refers to the manner in which the three persons of the Trinity relate to one

---

22. Eph. 2:18–22 (ESV).

23. Merriam-Webster Online, *Merriam-Webster Online Dictionary 2017,* s.v. "perichoresis," accessed August 14, 2017, https://www.merriam-webster.com/dictionary/perichoresis.

24. Alister E. McGrath, *Christian Theology: An Introduction,* 6th ed. (John Wiley and Sons, 2017), 305.

another. The concept of *perichoresis* allows the individuality of the persons to be maintained, while insisting that each person share in the life of the other two."[25] According to theo-semiotician Leonard Sweet, "God created us to be dancing partners, to join in the dance, to make the Trinity a quaternity, if you will, as we dance to the tune of Jesus,"[26] so that we are in God and God is in us.

THE DIVINE CONVERSATION

One of the ways we are invited and even commanded to interact with the members of the Godhead is through prayer, which is triune and prophetic in its essence, as Dr. Lee Roy Martin explains:

In prayer, we are experiencing the triune God, who acts triunely on us. Of course, we do not sense three presences....But we do sense that we are being joined in Christ to God's conversation with God. We find that we are not just speaking to God, but we are speaking with and for God, who is also speaking with and for us.[27]

God's conversation with God is captured in the psalms and quoted in Hebrews. Notice that Jesus is speaking to His Father, when He says, "I will proclaim Your name to My brethren, in the midst of the congregation I will sing your praise."[28] Today, Jesus sings to the Father through us as we enter what Sarah Coakley calls the "ceaseless divine dialogue." In it, we "are taken into the intra-Trinitarian 'place' of the Son. We pray Jesus'

25. Ibid.

26. Leonard Sweet, *So Beautiful: Divine Design for Life and the Church* (Colorado Springs: David C. Cook, 2009), 49.

27. Kimberly Ervin Alexander, "'Singing Heavenly Music': R. Hollis Gause's Theology of Worship and Pentecostal Experience," in *Toward a Pentecostal Theology of Worship*, ed. Lee Roy Martin (Cleveland, TN: CPT Press, 2016), 193–194.

28. Heb. 2:12, quoting Ps. 22:22.

prayer with him as the Spirit pressures us into him, freeing us for co-operation"[29] with him as he prays to the Father.

Christ in us enables us to pray. Jesus explained that "no one knows the Father except the Son and anyone to whom the Son chooses to reveal him."[30] Jesus revealed the Father and taught us to pray to him saying, "Our Father."[31] We often assume that these words address the One who is Father to us, our loved ones, the pastor, and the apostles. But Jesus was talking about our praying *with* Him to *His* Father, who is also our Father. What an exquisite invitation to join the ongoing conversation and draw from the mutual emptying between the Father and the Son!

Our reliance on Christ is imperative in prayer. "'For who has understood the mind of the Lord so as to instruct him?' But we have the mind of Christ."[32] Paul explained the role of the Holy Spirit in disseminating the divine understanding:

As it is written, "What no eye has seen, nor ear heard, nor the heart of man imagined, what God has prepared for those who love him"—these things God has revealed to us through the Spirit. For the Spirit searches everything, even the depths of God. For who knows a person's thoughts except the spirit of that person, which is in him? So also no one comprehends the thoughts of God except the Spirit of God.[33]

Paul also described how the Father searches both our hearts and the Spirit, as the Spirit simultaneously searches the Father's heart in order to intercede for us according to the

29. Chris E. W. Green, "'In Your Presence Is Fullness of Joy': Experiencing God as Trinity," in *Toward a Pentecostal* Lee Roy Martin, ed. *Theology of Worship* (Cleveland, TN: CPT, 2016), 194. Green draws from Rowan Williams, *On Christian Theology* (Malden, MA: Blackwell, 200), 124.

30. Matt. 11:27 (ESV).

31. Matt. 6:9–13.

32. 1 Cor. 2:16 (ESV).

33. 1 Cor. 2:9–11 (ESV). The idea that no eye has seen and no ear has heard has little to do with heaven; it is about who we are in Christ.

Father's will. The interplay highlights the preexistent peri-choresis to which we become party:

> *Likewise the Spirit helps us in our weakness. For we do not know what to pray for as we ought, but the Spirit himself intercedes for us with groanings too deep for words. And he who searches hearts knows what is the mind of the Spirit, because the Spirit intercedes for the saints according to the will of God. And we know that for those who love God all things work together for good, for those who are called according to his purpose.*[34]

As we are pulled into the triune exchange and the Spirit's intercession for us, the Father draws us toward "the measure of the stature of the fullness of Christ,"[35] so we can be and receive all that He desires.[36]

THE INVISIBLE REALM AND PROPHETIC IMAGINATION

Functioning as a charismatic and prophetic people means engaging the invisible and perceiving what is unimaginable to the natural mind. This is what Elijah and Elisha did, not with esoteric rituals, but with three essentials that Paul mentioned in the context of spiritual gifts. He wrote, "Now we see in a mirror dimly, but then face to face; now I know in part, but then I will know fully just as I also have been fully known. But now *faith, hope, love*, abide these three; but the greatest of these is love."[37]

The subject could fill another book, but in terms of our interaction with the invisible realm, we can say that

---

34. Rom. 8:26–28 (ESV).

35. Eph. 4:13.

36. This interpretation is based on Scripture and on Chris E. W. Green's piece, "'In Your Presence Is Fullness of Joy': Experiencing God as Trinity," in *Toward a Pentecostal* Lee Roy Martin, ed. *Theology of Worship* (Cleveland, TN: CPT, 2016).

37. 1 Cor. 13:12–13.

- faith is the art of *hearing* the invisible;
- hope is the art of *believing* the invisible;
- and love is the art of *trusting* the invisible.

This is how Elijah and Elisha penetrated the invisible realm to both perceive and participate in that which wanted to happen in fulfillment of God's will. They did not perform intellectual exercises to solve divine "riddles." They submitted themselves, intellect and all, to the pursuit of a God who desires to reveal Himself for the sake of His people and His eternal purpose.

Their example is important to us as modern-day sons of Issachar, especially in terms of our being expanded and drawn outside of perceived natural limitations. What they did is what we are called to do. In the face of death, they saw the possibility of raising the dead. When resources were nonexistent, they saw the possibility of unlimited supply. They saw these things, not with physical eyes but with spiritual ones.

This is not about conjuring or fantasizing. It is about prophetic imagination, the human imagination that is sanctified to perceive God's business in the invisible realm, and to believe and trust it. It is connected to our role as bearers of the divine *image*, as the word itself suggests. The sanctified imagination is the faculty of a person's inner environment (the mind). Not everyone acknowledges or exercises such a faculty. Therefore, what the prophets said seemed unimaginable to most hearers and only few people believed them. But those who humbled themselves eventually experienced what was promised.

Moses, Elijah, Elisha, Isaiah, Jeremiah, and others shared in the prophetic faculty of the sanctified imagination. By it, they accessed the invisible "place" from which their ministries flowed. Theologian Walter Brueggemann, author of *The Prophetic Imagination*, speaks in terms of alternative consciousness and offers this thesis: "The task of prophetic ministry is to nurture, nourish, and evoke a consciousness and perception alternative to the consciousness and perception of the dominant culture around us."[38]

Because the prophetic consciousness and perception are governed by God, they are by definition sanctified and alternative to the surrounding culture. In the current tech- and entertainment-oriented society, the disparity is more glaring. Our ability to imagine has been blunted by the continual bombardment of images which induce passivity and cause the imagination to atrophy.

The prophetic imagination is antithetical to passivity. The prophets of old were determined to obey God regardless of difficulty or disapproval in the community. Their obedience did not occur in a spiritual vacuum; their responses to the invisible manifested in the natural as they addressed people's needs. Elijah went to the widow of Zarephath who had already embraced a worst-case scenario: she would prepare a final meal, and then she and her son would die.[39] Her conclusion was not baseless. Drought had produced famine and death all around her. Hopelessness carried her to the emotional and intellectual space in which she could imagine only one outcome—the one she dreaded.

By faith Elijah heard God's voice in the invisible place and believed and trusted Him. He perceived an alternative future for the widow before its possibility was evident in the natural realm. Based on what he saw in his sanctified imagination, he made what would otherwise have been a reckless request: "Feed me first, then make something for you and your son to eat."[40] Imagine the blowback faced by a prophet making such a request in today's cultural and media environment!

---

38. Walter Brueggemann, *The Prophetic Imagination*, 2nd ed. (Minneapolis: Fortress Press, 201), 3.

39. 1 Kings 17.

40. 1 Kings 17:13.

Even the widow had her doubts; *but she obeyed* and received what the prophet offered. Centuries later, while speaking in a synagogue, Jesus honored her faith and contrasted her openness to the prophet with the apparent lack of receptivity in the prevailing culture:

> *There were many widows in Israel in the days of Elijah, when the sky was shut up for three years and six months, when a great famine came over all the land; and yet Elijah was sent to none of them, but only to Zarephath, in the land of Sidon, to a woman who was a widow.*[41]

Jesus knew His hearers were hampered by unsanctified imaginations and distorted expectations of Messiah. He had come to deliver them, but they imagined Him to be a threat. Unlike the widow, they forfeited the divine alternative and brought judgment upon themselves.

The widow's response to the charismatic prophet is the one for us to follow. Although she hesitated briefly, she quickly relented and embraced Elijah's offer. In the same way, our openness to Jesus's charismatic spirit opens us to alternative futures that can be revealed through prophecy, dreams, and visions. These revelations defy the accuser's claims that (1) there is only one available outcome, or (2) all available options are negative. This is the devil's proposed choice, but it is based on a closed system, his only source of information being the tree of the knowledge of good and evil. Barred from access to the tree of life, he cannot imagine divine alternatives.

We can, if we believe we can. That's the beauty of an open system: we get to choose. But we must realize when choosing that we get what we believe. Whatever our perception, it becomes our projection onto the future, and that becomes our reality. Whatever name or description we assign to a given situation, that is what it becomes. If we name it *dead, terrible,* or

---

41. Luke 4:25–26.

irreversible, God will respect our choice. He won't be in it, but He will honor it.

THIEVES IN THE INNER TEMPLE

Based on our interpretations of past experiences, we develop entire systems of preconceived notions, as the Pharisees did. When they compared the true Messiah in their midst to their false notions of what He "should" be, they reckoned Him a poseur. Instead of searching God's heart (hearing the invisible), they switched on the auto-pilot and made the worst possible miscalculation.

We are quick to decry their hardness of heart, but we also function on autopilot at least 70 percent of the time. Unconsciously, we deselect God's alternatives because they don't match our expectations and have become unimaginable to us.

We can become more consciously aware by asking ourselves the following questions often:

- Is this decision based on a closed system of expectations (a defiled imagination) or an open system in which my sanctified imagination perceives abundant alternative options?

- Do I habitually expect things to go from bad to worse, or do I typically expect positive outcomes?

Our answers can help us evict the thieves within.

NAAMAN'S BRUSH WITH THE INVISIBLE

Every believer has felt ignored by God at some point and wondered why his or her cries were not being heard. The truth is that we usually feel this way when we are doing the ignoring. It happens when we reject His divine alternatives to our situations, not intentionally, but effectively. The degree to which we dismiss His alternatives tends to directly correlate to the degree of our becoming desensitized to the invisible.

Naaman was a leper and formidable military leader whose disease was consuming him. According to Luke's Gospel, there "were many lepers in Israel in the time of Elisha the prophet; and none of them was cleansed, but only Naaman the Syrian."[42] How peculiar that he was the only leper healed. Why weren't there others, if not before Naaman, then afterward, as word of his healing got out?

Perhaps the story of Jesus and the lame man at the Pool of Bethesda can help explain the unhealed state of Naaman's contemporaries. Jesus knew the man at the pool had suffered for almost four decades, yet He asked, "Do you wish to get well?"[43] The man's answer would seem self-evident: "Of course I want to get well!"

Jesus knew the man's heart, and the man's answer confirmed it: "Sir, I have no man to put me into the pool when the water is stirred up, but while I am coming, another steps down before me."[44]

After decades of disability, the lame man was desensitized to aspects of the invisible. Therefore he rejected God's alternative, in essence declaring, "It's impossible for me to be healed."

Most lepers in Naaman's time made the same assessment. Naaman himself needed help getting to *yes*. The "valiant warrior"[45] was accustomed to power and victory. Yet his condition was winning. As a leader, he most likely kept it secret to avoid the embarrassment and isolation the disease imposed.

But a servant girl knew his secret and presented an alternative. She told Naaman's wife, "I wish that my master were with

42. Luke 4:27.
43. John 5:6.
44. John 5:7.
45. 2 Kings 5:1.

the prophet who is in Samaria! Then he would cure him of his leprosy."[46]

The servant was an Israelite taken captive in war. She might easily have resented her Syrian master, but she was a daughter of Abraham who understood her calling to bless all the nations of earth. She had nothing to offer him materially, but she offered the one thing he could not buy: a future.

She heard the invisible and then spoke it! Naaman caught the vision and pursued Elisha, but when Elisha spoke to him through a third party, he was insulted. Elisha compounded the insult by instructing Naaman to dip in the murky Jordan River seven times. Again, Naaman's servants intervened, urging him to obey Elisha's instructions. Naaman did, and he was healed.

How much more can we offer to our world as members in Christ's body? The ascended Son left us His mantle (His Spirit and Word), establishing an alternative community now numbering in the billions—and all of us called to operate in His charismatic and prophetic spirit.

PROPHESYING HOPE

Elijah and Elisha and their successor, Jesus, not only perceived alternative futures; they spoke them into being. This is not to say that God's prophets are immune to doubt. After Jezebel threatened his life, Elijah was wracked by fear and a suicidal spirit. Another prophet, Ezekiel, experienced the depths of hopelessness, as Israel did following centuries of division and ultimate exile. The psalmist captures the people's despair:

By the rivers of Babylon, there we sat down and wept, when we remembered Zion. Upon the willows in the midst of it we hung our harps. For there our captors demanded of us songs, and our tormentors' mirth, saying, "Sing us one of the

---

46. 2 Kings 5:3.

songs of Zion." How can we sing the LORD's song in a foreign land?[47]

Ezekiel did not hide his sorrow when God spoke to him in the valley of dry bones. Theologian Frank Macchia describes the scene:

Turn to Ezekiel 37 and see the prophet standing at the edge of a vast valley of dry bones. He has just been given a tour of the extent of the damage. The Lord has set him in the midst of the valley and led him back and forth, from one end to the other so that he could view how thoroughly lifeless Israel had become. [When]...the full extent of Israel's despair and hopelessness had settled into Ezekiel's heart and mind... the startling question came to him, "Son of man, can these bones live?"...Ezekiel answers in the only way that seems to make any sense at the moment: "O sovereign Lord, you alone know."[48]

God drew Ezekiel out of hopelessness by commanding him to prophesy an alternative future. He cooperated and God delivered. "The breath came into [the bones], and they came to life and stood on their feet, an exceedingly great army."[49] According to Macchia, the "Spirit of Yawheh had to be invoked before the new beginning was possible. Ezekiel is told to prophesy to the breath, a symbol of God's Spirit. Ezekiel bore witness to what happened"[50] as the bones "came to life and stood on their feet."[51]

Imagine the drama! But God did not raise the bones to be dramatic. Restoration served His kingdom purposes, which

47. Ps. 137:1–4.

48. Frank D. Macchia, *Justified in the Spirit: Creation, Redemption, and the Triune God* (Grand Rapids: William B. Eerdmans, 2010), 313.

49. Ezek. 37:10.

50. Macchia, *Justified in the Spirit*, 314.

51. Ibid.

included reviving the hope of His people. As Macchia explains, "Where there is no hope left, where all seems lost, where there is nothing but failure and death all around, God's breath offers the hope of redemption. The God of Israel, of the entire world, is known and vindicated as Lord precisely in this act of mercy and embrace through the Spirit of God."[52]

This is what God still longs to do. He has called us as a charismatic and prophetic people, a modern-day Issachar company, to perceive, speak, and release His glorious hope in the farthest corners of our disillusioned and despairing world.

By faith, we *imagine* it.

---

52. Ibid.

CHAPTER 6

THE KING OF GLORY AND HIS ANOINTING

As Jesus hung on the cross, His blood fell to the ground and began the process of redeeming His creation. It was a glorious accomplishment, but not exactly what His followers had in mind. Instead of seizing political and military dominance over Israel's enemies, the Savior humbled Himself and died an agonizing death. When it was over, He had taken back all dominion and every realm of authority. His anointing was beyond measure but it was not new; it was the same Spirit who brooded over the waters in Genesis 1—not an "energy" as some describe the Holy Spirit, but a Person.

The anointing flows from Christ, the Head, all through His body. These are the ones He promised would do "greater works"[1] than the ones He performed in His earthly walk. By God's design, we carry this treasure in our earthen vessels,[2] the unruly flesh, blood, and bone bodies the Creator chooses to use for His glory. Just as He ordained imperfect men like Moses, Joshua, Elijah, and Elijah, He has chosen us. And just as the mantle passed from Moses to Joshua and from Elijah to

---

1. John 5:20.
2. 2 Cor. 4:7.

Elisha, it has passed from Jesus to us, for the promise of greater works to be fulfilled.

What does God see in us? What promise do modern-day
sons and daughters of Issachar represent to the One who has
entrusted them with His Holy Spirit?

Perhaps it is what Jesus saw in a man named Nathanael who
sat under a fig tree: the working of the divine intent and purpose in a seeking human heart. Nathanael was a man without
guile, according to Jesus.[3] He wondered openly how a Naza-
rene could be the promised Savior, and then marveled at Jesus's ability to see him when it was physically impossible to do
so. So Jesus opened the horizons of Nathan's expectations:

*Jesus answered and said to him, "Because I said to you that I
saw you under the fig tree, do you believe? You will see greater things than these." And He said to him, "Truly, truly, I say
to you, you will see the heavens opened and the angels of God
ascending and descending on the Son of Man."*[4]

Jesus described to Nathanael His eventual ascension, in
which He would be lifted up into the cloud. He was preparing
Nathanael's heart to perceive what was to come. Elijah did the
same for Elisha when he told him to watch intently;[5] he prepared his protégé for a critical moment ahead. Jesus's ascension was more profound in its implications than Elijah's was,
but both Elisha and Jesus's disciples (and Jacob, at Bethel, for
that matter) witnessed the wonders of the heavenly realms.

As the disciples gazed "intently into the sky"[6] at the ascension, two angels in attendance asked them, "Men of Galilee,
why do you stand looking into the sky? This Jesus, who has

---

3. John 1:47.

4. John 1:50–51.

5. 2 Kings 2:10.

6. Acts 1:10.

been taken up from you into heaven, will come in just the same way as you have watched Him go into heaven."[7]

The angels spoke of the consummation that was being initiated then and would be finalized at the Second Coming. As Jesus ascended into glory, heaven and earth were reunited in the One who is Jacob's ladder. The new heaven and new earth had already begun with the New Man, and His followers could now be empowered from on high.

The Last Adam gave the Spirit without measure.[8] At Pentecost, the pouring out of His gift began. Through His disciples, Jesus started showing up in places He could not have reached in His physical body. The hope of glory was released in the earth: Christ was enthroned in the hearts of His redeemed.

EMBODIED SPIRITS

On the Day of Pentecost, the Holy Spirit brooded over humanity and poured Himself into the King's followers. The New Creation began with the Man in the Glory. He is the *Man* in the Glory because He arose *with* His physical body.

This is the New Creation model. God did not create us to be disembodied. Although many in the body of Christ long for heaven and the "liberation" of the human spirit from the physical body, the separation was never God's intent. It resulted from the Fall, which introduced us to death. Death is not the "friend" that takes us "home." Death is the "last enemy that will be abolished."[9]

---

7. Acts 1:11.

8. John 3:34.

9. 1 Cor. 15:26.

NEW CREATION AND THE DOUBLE PORTION

Fulfilling mission compels us to remember who we are—a regenerated people and a royal priesthood, the New Creation made possible by the Man in the Glory who was buried, descended, and ascended with His physical body. On the Day of Pentecost, His mantle fell and became our priestly garments. It was His plan: the Holy Spirit brooded over humanity and poured Himself into the King's followers!

When Elisha asked for the double portion he knew he was asking for an inheritance legally reserved for the firstborn. He also knew that he was called. His response to Elijah at Abel-meholah revealed his sense of readiness. He might not have expected exactly what happened, but Elisha was expecting *something* to happen, based on his sense of who he was. Elijah knew Elisha was God's chosen successor; but on the day of Elijah's departure to heaven, Elisha proved that he was the visionary prophet worthy to receive the mantle.

Jesus did not have to prove His status as "the firstborn of all creation" and "the firstborn among many brethren."[10] He received the inheritance and made us, the "general assembly and church of the firstborn,"[11] his joint-heirs, the "Elisha" to whom He promised a double portion.[12] What greater works could there be than the resurrection, except that Jesus, the Seed and true son of Issachar who understood the times, now works through millions and even billions around the globe?

Therefore, our mission is to follow Him. Throughout His earthly ministry, Jesus was *going somewhere*—not only to the cross, but also to His Father's right hand. Two thousand years later, Jesus is *still* going somewhere. The question is, "Are we going with Him?" The transfer of power between

---

10. Col. 1:15; Rom. 8:29.

11. Rom. 8:17; Heb. 12:23.

12. John 5:20.

Elijah and Elisha typified the transfer between Jesus and His disciples. However, the latter transfer is ongoing. Jesus is continually dropping His mantle on a fresh generation. If, like Elisha, they are sons and daughters of Issachar, they know where the mantle is falling and they are ever positioning themselves to catch it!

As long as we follow Jesus, we continue moving forward in power with signs and wonders following us. The greater works are not about following signs. We follow Him, and signs follow us. We have His mantle and are empowered to shift atmospheres. In that shifting, signs and wonders are released and witnessed.

JUDAH'S DONKEY AND THE LION

Jesus, the Lion of the Tribe of Judah, who was born in Bethlehem in the territory of Judah, grew up on Issachar's border, in Nazareth. In the perfect harmony of God's eternal purpose, Judah's donkey and Judah's Lion find their correlation in Jesus, the Judahite and "Issacharian" whose story is the ultimate fulfillment of Jacob's prophesy to Issachar in Genesis 49.

TRUST THE MANTLE

When Elisha received Elijah's mantle, he used it *immediately*. Although he seemed to experience fleeting uncertainty about whether God was with him, he was not at all confused about what the mantle meant or what his role was in using it.

Elisha trusted what he received. This is evident in his dealings with Naaman, the leprous warrior.[13] When Naaman's servant girl recommended that he see Elisha, Naaman pursued the prophet through royal channels. When he told his king that he wanted to meet with the prophet, the king

---

13. See 2 Kings 5.

contacted the king of Israel, who feared that the Aramean king was not trying to help a leper but trying to start another war with Israel.

Naaman moved in circles of military acumen and power, yet confusion and insecurity tainted the perception of Israel's king. It was Elisha, a man of the soil with no background or standing in diplomacy or military might, who understood and advanced the matter. Why? Because he knew who he was and trusted his mantle. "When Elisha heard that the king of Israel had torn his clothes, he sent word to the king, saying, 'Why have you torn your clothes? Now let him [Naaman] come to me, and he shall know that there is a prophet in Israel.'"[14]

Elisha discerned the issue accurately and reassured the king of Israel. In essence, he said, "Naaman's request does not concern you and is no threat to your kingdom. He is not your responsibility. Shifting atmospheres and healing the sick are not within your domain. The weight of that mantle falls to me. God has put His Word in my mouth. Leave this to me."

At his core, Elisha was settled in his role, clear about his assignment, and unafraid of powerful people. His dealings with Naaman show that titles did not impress him. Instead of meeting with Naaman personally, Elisha sent a messenger with a list of instructions. Adding insult to injury, the messenger Elisha sent was not a prophetic underling but a second-string servant!

Obviously, earthly airs and perks were of no interest to Elisha. When Naaman offered him lavish gifts of appreciation, Elisha refused them. To a man who saw into the heavenly realms and served the King of the universe, they meant nothing! Elisha was satisfied with his measure of rule. His mantle was tried and true. It was exactly what he asked from Elijah, and it was *enough*. He wanted nothing more and nothing less. His meat, to use Jesus's words, was to do the will of God and

---

14. 2 Kings 5:8.

facilitate whatever He desired.[15] Elisha was not interested in impressing the mighty or in meeting their expectations. His purpose was to satisfy the heart of God.

The mantle is about service, and servanthood is Issachar's heart. Remember that servants were instrumental in Naaman's healing. A captive servant girl turned Naaman's vision toward healing. Another servant convinced Naaman to humble himself and obey the prophet, despite the prophet's snubbing. And Elisha's own servant was used in Naaman's deliverance when he delivered the prophet's instructions.

Whatever their tribes, these servants typify what Jacob prophesied about Issachar as a strong donkey and a bearer of burdens. Sons and daughters of Issachar are never hapless, whatever their social standing. They are not kept in the dark but are anointed and privy to the times, knowing within themselves exactly what needs to be done.

Naaman's servants knew they were called to bless the nations. When Naaman was flummoxed, they shifted atmospheres and provided godly counsel. Without their interventions, even a powerful man like Naaman would not have been healed. But through their obedience, he was restored, physically and spiritually.

Their role is also ours: to be healing servants of the living God so that people can be delivered from whatever might be eating them alive. This is our priesthood. Signs will follow us as we believe and obey. The more willing we are as servants, the more God's anointing and alternatives will be revealed, so that we can offer the solutions the rest of the world fails to detect.

EMBRACING OUR PRIESTHOOD

We carry the mantle of the Son of God, and what a profound truth it is! In Ephesians chapter 1, we see the Man in the Glory

---

15. John 4:34.

who is prophet, priest, and king. In Ephesians chapter 2, we see ourselves seated with Him in heavenly places:

> *God, being rich in mercy, because of His great love with which He loved us, even when we were dead in our transgressions, made us alive together with Christ (by grace you have been saved), and **raised us up with Him, and seated us with Him in the heavenly places in Christ Jesus,** so that in the ages to come He might show the surpassing riches of His grace in kindness toward us in Christ Jesus.*[16]

He has raised us with Him because He was first raised, as Paul explains in Ephesians 1:19–23:

> *These [the hope of His calling, what are the riches of the glory of His inheritance in the saints, and what is the surpassing greatness of His power toward us who believe]*[17] *are in accordance with the working of the strength of His might which He brought about in Christ, when **He raised Him from the dead and seated Him at His right hand in the heavenly places, far above all rule and authority and power and dominion, and every name that is named,** not only in this age but also in the one to come. And He put all things in subjection under His feet, and gave Him as head over all things to the church, which is His body, the fullness of Him who fills all in all.*

We are the body, the fullness of Him, according to Paul. We are also His brethren who bear His image. This is God's work, not ours. As Elisha trusted his mantle, we are to trust who we are and what we are called to do. In our spiritual DNA, we are kings *and* priests, chosen by God. Paul said it this way:

> *You are A CHOSEN RACE, A royal PRIESTHOOD, A HOLY NATION, A PEOPLE FOR God's OWN POSSESSION, so that you may proclaim the excellencies of Him who has called you out of darkness*

---

16. Eph. 2:4–7.

17. Eph. 1:18–19.

into His marvelous light; for you once were NOT A PEOPLE, but now you are THE PEOPLE OF GOD; you had NOT RECEIVED MERCY, but now you have RECEIVED MERCY.[18]

We have much to do! Notice that we are a *royal* priesthood, invested with a measure of rule. In our priestly capacity, we attend to the business of calling that which is in heaven into earthly manifestation. This is the binding and loosing that brings the earthly realm into agreement with heaven's reality. Our conduct is not hesitant or apathetic, like those who are slaves to the prevailing currents. We are a people actively engaged because we understand and embrace our measure of rule *over those prevailing currents.*

The priesthood of God's people is not strictly a New Testament reality. Notice God's instruction long before the Incarnation:

Moses went up to God, and the LORD called to him from the mountain, saying, "Thus you shall say to the house of Jacob and tell the sons of Israel: 'You yourselves have seen what I did to the Egyptians, and how I bore you on eagles' wings, and brought you to Myself. 'Now then, if you will indeed obey My voice and keep My covenant, then you shall be My own possession among all the peoples, for all the earth is Mine; and **you shall be to Me a kingdom of priests and a holy nation**.*' These are the words that you shall speak to the sons of Israel."*[19]

The Israelites were liberated from slavery and called into God's priesthood. Their deliverance was profound; but ours, as rendered through the cross, is more profound, as the early Church fathers understood. They grasped how radical the change was, and they understood God's enormous investment of power in the Church.

---

18. 1 Pet. 2:9–10.
19. Exod. 19:3–6.

Are we as aware? Or are we prone to overlooking or taking for granted that which the early Church took to heart? The Reformation emphasized the priesthood of all believers and helped to restore the early Church understanding of it. Now, five centuries later, will the privilege of our priesthood compel us to walk boldly in our mission? And will we enter the prophethood of all believers?

THE HEAVENLY COUNCIL

Our role in the earthly realm hinges upon our standing in heavenly places. If this truth is dulled, we inevitably lose sight of something Scripture plainly describes: God's heavenly council. This is the "war room" of which the psalmist said, "God has taken his place in the divine council; in the midst of the gods he holds judgment."[20]

The council existed long before the psalmist wrote of it. In fact, the book of Job mentions a pre-Adamic angelic council, writing, "Now there was a day when the sons of God came to present themselves before the LORD, and Satan [literally, *the Satan*] also came among them."[21]

Some scholars believe that the twenty-four thrones of the ancient ones depicted in Revelation 4 and 5 are also part of the council. It is possible that when God said, ""Let Us make man in Our image, according to Our likeness,"[22] that He was speaking not only among the members of the Godhead, but also to angelic members of His court.

God's friend, Abraham, was in the council and heard things that other men and women were not privileged to hear. Before God judged Sodom and Gomorrah, He said, "Shall I hide from Abraham what I am about to do, since Abraham will surely

---

20. Ps. 82:1 (ESV).

21. Job 1:6. "The Satan" was not cast out of heaven until Christ rose and ascended to heaven.

22. Gen. 1:26.

become a great and mighty nation, and in him all the nations of the earth will be blessed?"[23]

Remember that Abraham did not live in Sodom or Gomorrah; Lot did. Yet Abraham was informed, and Lot was not. It is likely because Lot was not in God's council. Neither were the people in his city. Therefore, they did not know what would befall them. But God told Abraham, who drove a hard bargain with God until he gained from Him the assurance that Lot and his family would not perish in the destruction of Sodom and Gomorrah.[24] Notice that God did not reprimand Abraham for his persistence. Pleading the case with God was entirely appropriate for a member of the council.

Consider also Enoch, who "walked with God."[25] How could he have walked with God when the Edenic sanctuary was guarded by a flaming sword? Perhaps it was because Enoch was a council member. We know that he had inside information in advance of the great flood. He knew that when his son, Methuselah died, an epic flood would come. So, he prepared four generations of his progeny (including Noah, who was also in the council) for what was ahead.

Through Noah, God would restore and rebuild the human population on the earth. When Noah was instructed to build an ark on dry land, the assignment did not take him by surprise. He had been raised with the knowledge of a coming flood, through Enoch's revelation of faith—the revelation which also enabled him to pass safely through the flaming sword that was designed to keep humans out. And when Enoch's earthly work was done, he simply passed out of this dimension and into the next, without tasting death.

---

23. "Gen. 18:17–18.

24. Gen. 18:23–32.

25. Gen. 5:24

Others, including Elijah, Elisha, and Isaiah entered the council. Today, God's royal priesthood are members of the divine council. People outside the faith, and even some within the Church, bristle at the thought of human beings having access to heavenly realms. Yet this is God's design. The Last Adam restored to us what the First Adam threw away: the right to rule and reign over God's Creation!

To the extent that we fail to embrace this reality, we exchange the truth for a lie.[26] In the distortion of natural human thinking, we might presume that it is humble to disclaim our heavenly status. In reality, to deny it is to commit idolatry. Instead of looking up to God in faith and in recognition of whose we are, we would be relinquishing our place by looking down to the dust and despising the image we were created to bear.

If the divine council still seems like a "foreign" idea, consider this: Everything in the kingdom of darkness is a counterfeit of the divine original. If all of mythology is structured around pantheons of gods (which it is), then it is also modeled after an original. That original is the divine council, God's holy pantheon.

The divine council is an active place. According to Psalms 81:1, God holds judgment in the midst of the gods, the *elohim* or angelic majesties. Scripture says we are also *elohim*. Jesus publicly endorsed this idea while answering those He offended with His claim to be the Son of God. He made His case by quoting Psalms 82:6, which speaks to God's people, saying the following: "I said, 'You are *gods*, and all of you are sons of the Most High.'" The word translated "gods" is *elohim*.

Clearly, God's investment of authority in His people is intentional. We are His royal priesthood and members of His council. However, our membership does not guarantee our full and effective participation there. Being active in the council

---

26. Rom. 1:25.

depends upon (1) our ability to believe who we are, and (2) our decision to take our places in God's grand scheme.

This requires maturity. All believers are complete in Christ; but not all are mature. As the writer of Hebrews explained: "Solid food is for the mature, who because of practice have their senses trained to discern good and evil."[27] Mature believers take their places in the council, not proudly but confidently. When they pray, they do not ask for their opinions or preferences to be carried out. They subject their desires to the divine will, and they pray prayers that God longs to answer! Therefore, God confides in them the way He confided in Abraham, and they walk with Him as Enoch did.

A stark narrative in the book of Zechariah reveals the council and the working relationship between God and His council members. In the account, Joshua the high priest, Zechariah the prophet, and Satan stand before the Lord during a very high-stakes period for God's people. In the natural sense, Davidic rule was interrupted and the monarchy was lost. The people were in exile. The temple was in ruins. In terms of legitimacy, the temple project and the priesthood were at risk. As a council member, Zechariah understood the seriousness of the times and told the story within that context.

> *Then he showed me Joshua the high priest standing before the angel of the Lord, and Satan standing at his right hand to accuse him. The Lord said to Satan, "The Lord rebuke you, Satan! Indeed, the Lord who has chosen Jerusalem rebuke you! Is this not a brand plucked from the fire?" Now Joshua was clothed with filthy garments and standing before the angel.*[28]

"Filthy garments" is a polite way of saying that Joshua was covered in excrement. As the high priest charged with representing God's people, Joshua's degraded condition signifies

27. Heb. 5:14.

28. Zech. 3:1–3.

the their diminished state. It also foreshadows the Great High Priest who would be clothed in the filth of all humanity and beaten to a bloody pulp before defeating every ungodly principality and power and overcoming every evil thing.

Not surprisingly, Satan seized upon the moment to accuse Joshua before God. Although Joshua's condition was not fitting for a man in his position, God did not lash out against him. Instead, He rebuked Satan and restored His high priest.

He spoke and said to those who were standing before him, saying, "Remove the filthy garments from him." Again he said to him, "See, I have taken your iniquity away from you and will clothe you with festal robes." **Then I said, "Let them put a clean turban on his head."** *So they put a clean turban on his head and clothed him with garments, while the angel of the LORD was standing by.*[29]

Notice the interaction and how Zechariah chimed into the conversation, adding to God's instructions by requesting a clean turban for the high priest. Does the prophet's input seem too forward or presumptuous? It might, but only if we misunderstand our Father's intent. He *called* Zechariah into service, and He has called us. The council is open to us; why would we disqualify ourselves and others from participating there?

Zechariah's boldness reveals the confident participation of a council member who recognizes his calling and is in agreement with the divine plan. God raised no objection to Zechariah's input, which was in keeping with His own desire to restore the priest. Instead, He allowed the prophet's instruction to be carried out as stated.

We are blood-bought, anointed members of the divine council who function under a new and better covenant.[30] We are seated in heavenly places with the King of Glory, to be part

29. Zech. 3:4–5.

30. Heb. 7:22; 12:24.

of heaven's "business." What the Lord said to Joshua is also for us:

> *Thus says the LORD of hosts, "If you will walk in My ways and if you will perform My service, then you will also govern My house and also have charge of My courts, and I will grant you free access among these who are standing here."*[31]

The King of Glory has anointed sons and daughters of Issachar for great works.

---

31. Zech. 3:7.

CHAPTER 7

RESTORING THE CITY, REBUILDING THE CULTURE

THE COMMISSION OF GOD'S VANGUARD company is to understand the times and to know what to do. The first part is often clearer than the second. The Church is largely in touch with the times but often at a loss for what to do about them.

During cultural crises, this disconnect becomes painfully evident. Remember the gulf that separated the sons of Issachar from other leaders as the house of Saul yielded to the house of David. Centuries later, a chasm opened between those who recognized the Incarnate Son and those who rejected Him. God's plan was again fulfilled, pleasing some and infuriating others.

Both events culminated in God's desired restoration. In David, the devotion to divine rule was restored when God's man took the throne. When Jesus's work was completed, the power of sin was broken, the King served notice to every realm of authority, and the restoration of the new heaven and new earth began. After His ascension, Jesus transferred His mantle to the Church, which became His chosen instrument of recovery.

For two thousand years, the Church has facilitated restoration in cities, nations, and cultures. Today, the city in need of restoration is the city of God, the Church itself, which has largely exchanged its kingdom culture for the culture of the world.

The city must be restored, and its kingdom culture must be rebuilt.

RESTORING GOD'S INSTRUMENT OF RECOVERY

Cultural crises are not new. Since the first century, the Church has stood firm as an anchor and restorative force amid crooked and perverse generations. The question now is whether the Church is still prepared for its mission. Having largely acquiesced to a culture of celebrity in which worship is confused with cultural ecstasy, the answer is uncertain. We must decide whether we will own our condition and embrace restoration, break from culturally- and politically-correct postures, and recover the distinctives that made the Church *the Church.*

Only God can restore His Church, and only with our buy-in. Despite the fraying of our fabric, we are bound together in covenant with the Last Adam. *We are still His body!* By His rising, He produced offspring in the four corners of the earth—a resilient and divinely-appointed family against which the gates of hell cannot prevail.[1] The world's persecuted churches, in environments as harsh as Iran's and China's, remind us that His Church will one day be the Church of His dreams.

The vibrancy of the persecuted Church is not yet seen everywhere. In the West, for example, the Church is largely preoccupied with "prophetic" conspiracy theories and escapist longings that demotivate and neutralize its effectiveness. Interpreting Scripture through the grid of current events is unbiblical and cannot answer the world's woes. Arguments over

---

1. See Matt. 16:18.

the Church's departure—whether it is imminent, far off, or not to be—serve only to distract us from our work.

Our true calling is to be the Church militant, occupying until He comes and emptying heaven's treasures into this earthly realm. We received the anointing, His Holy Spirit, not to flee a collapsing culture, but to be Jesus' hands and feet in the midst of crisis. The Holy Spirit has given us His grace gifts as our tools. They are not intended to create "buzz" or to promote the spectacular; they are meant to be used effectively and generously by those who understand the times and know what to do about them.

BREAKPOINTS

In the Church, as in the world, cycles of restoration and rebuilding are linked to key junctures or *breakpoints* in history. An important part of understanding the times is being able to identify these breakpoints and recognize the changes they portend. Though all cultures change from generation to generation and millennium to millennium, breakpoints are standout periods having common features. The apostle Paul described those features two thousand years ago:

Even though they knew God, they did not honor Him as God or give thanks, but they became futile in their speculations, and their foolish heart was darkened. Professing to be wise, they became fools, and exchanged the glory of the incorruptible God for an image in the form of corruptible man and of birds and four-footed animals and crawling creatures. Therefore God gave them over in the lusts of their hearts to impurity, so that their bodies would be dishonored among them. For they exchanged the truth of God for a lie, and worshiped and served the creature rather than the Creator, who is blessed forever. Amen. For this reason God gave them over to degrading passions; for their women exchanged the natural function for that which is unnatural, and in the same way also the men abandoned the natural function of the woman and burned in their desire toward one another, men with men committing indecent acts and receiving in their own persons the due penalty of their error. And just as they did not see fit to acknowledge God any longer, God gave them over to a depraved mind, to do those things which are not proper.[2]

Could there be a more apt description of our twenty-first century world? Depravity is rampant. God is not worshipped. His truth has been exchanged for lies. Moral restraint is out of vogue. Narcissism is prevalent. Violence is ubiquitous. Evil is called good and good is called evil.

As bleak a litany as it seems, the potential for transformation is enormous. The current breakpoint is a *kairos* moment, an interruption and disruption that demands our response. How we respond determines where the breakpoint will lead. When we understand the times, know what to do, and do it (as the sons of Issachar did in the Saul-to-David transition), our breakpoint leads to breakthrough. If we respond with indecision, impulse, or inaction, our breakpoints produce breakdowns. Either way, the resulting change is momentous.

Breakpoints are about endings and beginnings. The house of Saul ended, and the house of David arose. The ministry of Elijah yielded, and the ministry of Elisha ensued. The Aaronic priesthood gave way to the Melchizedek order of our Great High Priest. Uncertainty marked each of these transitions:

- The sons of Issachar recognized David's kingship but could not know all that lay ahead of him and the nation.

- Elisha knew within himself that he was called, but did not know precisely when the transition would come or whether God would back him as He backed Elijah (hence his question, "Where is the LORD, the God of Elijah?"). Even the successful transfer of the mantle was not automatic but required Elisha's decision to receive, which set

---

2. Rom. 1:21–28.

in motion a trajectory that would not have existed otherwise.

- The changing of the priestly order disrupted the status quo, upended Judaic traditions, and demanded of God's people a willingness to perceive afresh.

Five hundred years after Martin Luther nailed his 95 theses to the cathedral door, we have arrived at another breakpoint. In an era of profound disillusionment and godlessness, we are called to the trajectory Jesus is on. His divine vision is to release salvation throughout His Creation. This is more than deliverance from sin; it is the release from constricted places into open spaces of generosity and prosperity, as modeled by the exodus from Egyptian slavery and the entrance into the land of milk and honey. Included in this vision is God's *shalom*, where nothing is missing or broken, every beneficial thing is present, and everything harmful is absent.

This is the future *from which* and *into which* Jesus is calling His Church.

SPIRITUAL SIGHT, MATURITY, AND FOUNDATION

As a prophetic people, the Issachar company is a *seeing* people who perceive opportunities for restoration and rebuilding. They see what everyone else sees—upheaval, uncertainty, amorality—but they interpret these signs differently. Where others focus on lack and doom, the sons and daughters of Issachar see possibility and alternative outcomes.

This is spiritual sight, which involves understanding what is behind that which is seen. Spiritual sight perceives signs but goes further; it makes meaning by transforming signs into significance. When we use spiritual sight, we discern the sign's purpose and declare its meaning for the benefit of others. This is what the sons of Issachar did in David's day. They recognized the signs of their times and understood that they signified a shift in Israel's leadership. They discerned the implications of that shift and declared God's intentions so that those over whom they had influence could embrace what God was doing.

Just as a prophetic people are called to speak beyond themselves, spiritual sight requires us to see beyond ourselves into what God is doing. (How can we embrace what we do not see?) In our "What's in it for me?" culture where sight is filtered through the lens of desire and comfort, spiritual sight requires the same maturity that compels us to take our places in God's grand scheme. This maturity not only thrusts us forward but can also preserve us from falling away.[3]

True spiritual sight guards against such dangers, merging our insights (the intuitive knowledge that comes from within) with our "outsights" (the empirical knowledge we can verify by observation). The melding of the two produces what can be called *depth sight*. This is a level of meaning-making by which we identify patterns and connect dots in order to see the unseen, hear the unheard, and speak the unspoken (see Chapters 4 and 5).

The maturity that supports spiritual sight also supports a healthy sense of time within the context of eternity. As a covenant people, we do not live in the past; but neither should we discard it. We can instead value our history as a people, drawing from the past that which is also part of the future. Our cause is not to reinvent the faith, but to contend "for the faith *that was once for all delivered to the saints.*"[4] This is the *regula fidei*, the rule of faith embodied in the creeds we have confessed for centuries. Fidelity to our ancient foundations is not reactionary; it inoculates us against spurious doctrines and revisionist theologies that pander to the human appetite for "something new."

Though we value our history as a people, we are drawn into the future *from the future*, where Jesus, our forerunner, already is:

---

3. See Heb. 6:1-6.

4. Jude 3.

This hope we have as an anchor of the soul, a hope both sure and steadfast and one which enters within the veil, where Jesus has entered as a forerunner for us, having become a high priest forever according to the order of Melchizedek.[5]

In this passage, the word translated *forerunner* depicts our Savior forging the way through great sacrifice. When ancient vessels in rough seas attempted to drop anchor near the shore, they risked being wrecked among the rocks. Therefore, a forerunner was appointed to swim ahead through churning waters, risking life and limb to protect the ship and safely drop anchor. The forerunner then used every ounce of his strength to pull the ship into its destined resting place.

Our divine forerunner's work is perfect, but the future into which He draws us is rarely convenient. Jesus often leads by inconvenience to places we never expected or desired to go. That is what happened when God sent Elijah to find his successor in Abel-meholah. The name of the place suggests joy, hope, and a belief in the future, a state totally other than Elijah's depressive frame of mind. Elijah did not fit in Elisha's environment. Yet, fulfilling the plan of God required him to go there.

Places and even people can be inconvenient. So are our beliefs. In the current culture, the truth is becoming unwelcome. Yet the truth must continue to be our standard. The world mocks truth, and us with it, calling us old-fashioned and unsympathetic to their needs and desires. They label us *fools* and deride our way of life. Yet, like the apostle Paul, we gladly choose to be "fools" for Christ's sake.

To function as a vanguard company, we must expect reproach. We are privileged to "go to him outside the camp and bear the reproach he endured."[6]

---

5. Heb. 6:19–20. This describes a change from the Aaronic priesthood.

6. Heb. 13:13 (ESV).

RESTORATION IN HISTORY AND METAPHOR

Restoration and rebuilding are part of biblical history. When Israel seemed hopelessly divided and idolatry became increasingly pervasive, Elijah took a stand, challenging 850 prophets of Baal and Ashtoreth. The situation was so dire that Elijah thought he was alone in serving God. His assessment of the culture was accurate, but his sense of being the *only* remaining prophet was self-centric and incorrect.

Others served God, no doubt sharing Elijah's hopes of restoration and rebuilding. While Elijah prophesied against Ahab and Jezebel from outside the royal court, God's prophet, Obadiah, served from the inside. Imagine a true prophet serving Ahab and Jezebel as they boasted of murdering God's people! Working in such proximity to His enemies, Obadiah risked his life daily. Yet he faithfully protected endangered prophets, hiding them from Jezebel and providing for their sustenance.

By this time, places such as Gilgal, Bethel, Jericho, and Ai had become infected with Baal worship, which continued even after Elijah's showdown at Mount Carmel.[7] Recovering from his suicidal rant under the broom tree, Elijah returned to the fight against idolatry, founding the schools of the prophets in the very places where Baal worship was flourishing.

Remember that in Joshua's day, places like Gilgal, Jericho, and Ai were key points of entry into the Promised Land, with Jericho being the site of the Israelites' first and perhaps most stunning victory. Now, hundreds of years later, Jericho languished under the curse Joshua declared against anyone who attempted to rebuild the city:

Joshua made them take an oath at that time, saying, "Cursed before the LORD is the man who rises up and builds this city Jericho; with the loss of his firstborn he shall lay

---

7. This was not the same Bethel where Jacob saw a ladder to heaven. This Bethel was north of Ai.

its foundation, and with the loss of his youngest son he shall set up its gates."[8]

By the time Elisha received the prophet's mantle, Joshua's command had been defied, with devastating consequences:

In [Ahab's] days Hiel the Bethelite built Jericho; he laid its foundations with the loss of Abiram his firstborn, and set up its gates with the loss of his youngest son Segub, according to the word of the LORD, which He spoke by Joshua the son of Nun.[9]

Not only had Hiel's sons perished, but the city's water supply was toxic. Hoping for their city and people to be restored to health, men of Jericho approached Elisha, saying, "Behold, the situation of this city is pleasant, as my lord sees, but the water is bad, and the land is unfruitful."[10]

Elisha, a true son of Issachar, understood the issue and its ramifications and knew precisely what to do:

He said, "Bring me a new bowl, and put salt in it." So they brought it to him. Then he went to the spring of water and threw salt in it and said, "Thus says the Lord, I have healed this water; from now on neither death nor miscarriage shall come from it." So the water has been healed to this day, according to the word that Elisha spoke.[11]

In the Hebrew, to say the "situation [was] pleasant,"[12] revealed something more. The word translated "situation" is *mosab*, which means "seat, assembly...sitting company."[13] An

---

8. Josh. 6:26.

9. 1 Kings 16:34.

10. 2 Kings 2:19.

11. 2 Kings 2:20–22.

12. 2 Kings 2:19.

13. Francis Brown, Samuel Rolles Driver, and Charles Augustus Briggs, *Enhanced Brown-Driver-Briggs Hebrew and English Lexicon* (Oxford: Clarendon Press, 1977), s.v. "mosab," H4186.

assembly is a group of people gathered together for a shared purpose. The word pictures Jericho, not as a collection of residents, but as an assembly of people gathered with purpose.

Because the water was malignant, the assembly suffered. Death prevailed and babies spontaneously aborted from their mothers' wombs. The land miscarried crops, and men and women were rendered sterile and barren. Bad water poisoned the physical environment and crushed the people's dreams.

The story is rich with references to restoration. When Elisha requested a new bowl, he literally asked for a *renewed* bowl. This would have been a bowl once used in service to God, subsequently rendered useless through damage or disuse, and ultimately restored by being purged in the fire and remolded. This is the specially prepared instrument Elisha would use to renew and reform a cursed place. In addition, salt, a preservative that was also used in offerings, was added to the bowl.

This is a powerful metaphor of the Church! To the degree that we have surrendered the characteristics that mark us as the people of God and of His Spirit, we poison ourselves, abort our purpose, and lose sight of His intent. As the city of God and the salt of the earth, we must be restored so a new generation can carry on God's purpose and remain as Christ's incarnational presence in the earth.

Transformation and reformation begin with the Church. To be God's instrument of recovery and restoration means first becoming acutely aware that we "were born, not of blood nor of the will of the flesh nor of the will of man, but of God."[14] Having common spiritual origins, we are called to move as one, an assembly empowered to restore and rebuild what has been poisoned, knowing that even the increasing darkness is emblematic of the increasing brightness to come.

---

14. John 1:13.

AUTHORITY BY DESIGN

Restoring the city (the Church) and rebuilding the culture is a work of and by the Spirit, effected through God's instrument of recovery, the Church. It is an act of emptying into our midst all the treasures of heaven, as those who have access to those treasures and authority to transfer them.

We are a people of dual residency: we live on the earth and are seated in heavenly places. The apostle Paul explained that our seating is by God's invitation and design.[15] Our being raised up with Christ is possible because our Prophet, Priest, and King, was first raised from the dead and seated at the Father's right hand, as Paul explains:

He [God] *raised Him* [Jesus] *from the dead and seated Him at His right hand in the heavenly places, far above all rule and authority and power and dominion, and every name that is named, not only in this age but also in the one to come. And He put all things in subjection under His feet, and gave Him as head over all things to the church, which is His body, the fullness of Him who fills all in all.*[16]

God's kingdom designs are purposeful. As Elijah went before Elisha, Jesus Christ went before us. He was seated on high and we are seated with Him, enthroned with Him in kingly authority. The question is *why*? Why are we given access to such high places? What is the purpose of our being there?

In essence, the "war room" or council from which God rules and reigns is a place of worship and praise. But it is also the ultimate seat of power and authority. Throughout history, God has used members of His council as instruments of recovery. For example, Moses delivered the Israelites; Noah built the ark for the salvation of the human race; Elisha removed the curse from Jericho, whose water remains potable to this day.

---

15. Eph. 2:4–7.
16. Eph. 1:20–23.

Now, God's redeemed serve in His council so that we might effectively exercise our dominion, inquire of Him, receive our orders, and be equipped and empowered to facilitate His unfolding plan.

THRONES AND WAR

Thrones are a sign of kingly authority. Inevitably, thrones are also for war. Warfare is required to "occupy until He comes." This includes the Church's work as His instrument of recovery. Our efforts to restore the city and rebuild the culture will be resisted, but to the victors will go the spoils.

In Christ, the kingdom has come, and is still coming. We are not called to an eschatology of defeat by which we passively wait for the lion and lamb to dwell together in peace. As "A CHOSEN RACE, A royal PRIESTHOOD, A HOLY NATION, A PEOPLE FOR God's OWN POSSESSION... [we] may proclaim the excellencies of Him who has called [us] out of darkness into His marvelous light; for [we] once were NOT A PEOPLE, but now [we] are THE PEOPLE OF GOD; [we] had NOT RECEIVED MERCY, but now [we] have RECEIVED MERCY.[17]

Having received mercy, the sons and daughters of Issachar also carry God's mercy to the world.

THE CITY OF GOD

We are to restore the city of God, which is Christ's Church. It has several scriptural names and appears in type and shadow in the Old Testament. It is the same city for which faithful Abraham searched:

---

17. 1 Pet. 2:9–10.

By faith [Abraham] *lived as an alien in the land of promise, as in a foreign land, dwelling in tents with Isaac and Jacob, fellow heirs of the same promise; for he was looking for the city which has foundations, whose architect and builder is God.*[18]

In Hebrews 12, the city is also called Zion, the "general assembly and church of the firstborn." Mount Zion, the city of the redeemed, is contrasted with Mount Sinai, where Moses was "full of fear and trembling":[19]

But you have come to Mount Zion and to the city of the living God, the heavenly Jerusalem, and to myriads of angels, to the general assembly and church of the firstborn who are enrolled in heaven, and to God, the Judge of all, and to the spirits of the righteous made perfect, and to Jesus, the mediator of a new covenant, and to the sprinkled blood, which speaks better than the blood of Abel.[20]

John the revelator also describes the city in Revelation chapter 21 as the glorious city that comes down from heaven as the temple city. As John explains, it fills the earth with the glory of God:

I saw no temple in it, for the Lord God the Almighty and the Lamb are its temple. And the city has no need of the sun or of the moon to shine on it, for the glory of God has illumined it, and its lamp is the Lamb. The nations will walk by its light, and the kings of the earth will bring their glory into it. In the daytime (for there will be no night there) its gates will never be closed; and they will bring the glory and the honor of the nations into it; and nothing unclean, and no one who prac-

---

18. Heb. 11:9–10.

19. Heb. 12:21.

20. Heb. 12:22–24.

THE DEAD PROPHETS SOCIETY

tices abomination and lying, shall ever come into it, but only those whose names are written in the Lamb's book of life.[21]

Imagine a city illumined by God's glory, where the gates never close and nothing unclean approaches! This is the city we are becoming, God's city, the Church of Jesus Christ. We are His prophetic witness to principalities and powers, so "that the manifold wisdom of God might now be made known through the church to the rulers and the authorities in the heavenly places."[22]

No wonder our gathering together is sacred! Our unity and faithfulness are critical to the cause of Christ. The restoration initiated with His sacrifice is ongoing through God's chosen instrument of recovery. When the work is completed, only one city will be left standing, the city of God, His community of diverse but interdependent people brought together in the shed blood of Christ and bound together, not in the culture of the world or even of our churches, but in the culture of heaven itself.

Let the recovery begin. It is time for the sons and daughters of Issachar to pursue God's vision, overtake, and recover all![23]

---

21. Rev. 21:22–27.

22. Eph. 3:10.

23. See 1 Sam. 30:8.

140